I dedicate this book to my *[illegible]* family *[illegible]* & Kaitlynn, who inspire me to be a better human every day.

Also, to my Mom and Dad. I think my favorite quote of my Dad's really applies to this time in history: "If money can fix your problems, then you don't have any."

# CONTENTS

# FORWARD

I believe that everyone should write a book. From the time I was very young, I would journal every day. So when my son Bryce said, "Mom you should write a book," I thought, why not?

At my cabin at the lake, last July, I started writing down ideas. They flowed so fast I had to jot them down as bullet points. I filled page after page, and even had to use the margins and write sideways to get them all in.

A few days later my friend, Daniel, texted me and said, "I think you should write a book". Well, funny enough, I had all the ideas written down already. I worked off and on at the book, but the major push came when I was at "Success Builders"; a group held at Home Church. They challenged the group to do something every day for 50 days, and there were prizes for those that succeeded. So, my goal was to write every day for 50 days, and in that time I was able to finish writing most of this book.

Then my wonderful content editor, Kalyn,and my wife, Darlene, finalized the copy edits. Even though it's taken longer than anticipated to get the book launched, with the coronavirus still on the scene I think the timing is perfect. My hope in writing the book is to entertain, encourage, enlighten, and educate – about Real Estate, but mainly about how to be happy and find joy no matter the circumstance. I find that with all the heaviness of COVID-19 and the total disruption in people's lives, the world could use a small dose of positive encouragement. I think everyone can use a laugh and maybe a new perspective on how to see things, especially in hard times.

I was in Hawaii on my winter holiday when we were strongly encouraged by the government to come home.

Our first flight was only 20% full, and many people were wearing masks. That particular flight from Kauai to Maui had very few people on it, but when we hit Maui, it was insane. There was a line about a quarter of a mile long of people waiting to get through security. It turned out that we had booked our tickets for the very last flight that would go out of Maui with WestJet.

A weird, sad, angry feeling permeated the airport. I told Darlene I wanted to wear my snorkel mask. It has a full face and the snorkel goes out the top. (Now, they have actually developed a protective mask using this same idea. So I'm not crazy, I'm creative). I was going to wear my bright yellow rubber gloves along with the snorkel mask. I really wanted to do it to make at least a few people smile. I thought some comic relief was in order.

I live my life trying to make people smile and to cheer them up. I hope and pray that you will find encouragement, inspiration, and maybe a little bit of laughter at the crazy and unexpected events that have transpired in my life.

Here's to a new perspective!


Aloha,


Penny

# 1 GERBIL LOOSE IN THE OFFICE

My love affair with real estate began when I was only 17.

My best friend's mom was a Realtor, and when I went over to her house, I would page through all the listings of homes for sale in her mom's magic black book. I was intrigued by all the different types of homes and loved leafing through this "secret" book.

Fast forward to Career Day in grade 12. Alan Edwards was the head of the Red Deer and District Real Estate Association, and the lucky duck who got to talk to our school about being a Realtor. I attended his presentation and waited patiently until the Q&A session. My question was simple:

"How do you find business?"

His reply – although short and succinct – still rings true: "*Ask everyone you meet and everyone you know if they want to buy or sell a house.*"

Well, that sounded easy. Years later, I now have to explain this to my kids. After being asked in an elevator one day by my young son, "Mom, do you have to talk to everyone?" I replied, "Well, yes honey, I do."

I refer to this as my *5 foot rule* – though, truthfully, it's grown to about 10 feet now. If anyone gets within 5 feet of me, my natural response is to talk to them. So this made the 'ask everyone you meet and everyone you know if they want to buy or sell a house' mantra fairly easy for me.

A year after the Alan Edwards presentation at Career Day, I met a friend who had just gotten her real estate license. I said to her, "Gee, I wish I was 21 so I could be a Realtor", and she replied that I only had to be 18. Wide-eyed, I asked how to go about it.

She directed me to the Real Estate Board where I paid my $250 for the Big-Bird-Yellow coloured binder containing the course that would turn me into a licensed Realtor.

I studied for about two weeks, then went in and took my exam. I remember going into the room filled with an assortment of people – everyone older, of course. One fellow in particular stood out as he looked about 80 to me, but at 18 everyone looked old, so he was probably only 60. Alan Hodge was his name. I found out later that he had taken the test three times and failed each time before this.

I started into the test, which was to take two hours. In less than an hour, I was done. I looked around... Alan Hodge was still on page 2! Then I looked at everyone else – they all had their heads down, studiously working on their exams. I thought *maybe I missed some pages,* so I reread the whole exam again, checking my work. *Yep, I was done, alright.*

I got up to walk to the front of the room to hand in my test. All eyes in the room shot up: "What's happening? Did she quit? She can't be done?" I headed home to wait about 10 days to receive the results.

In the mail came the answer: "YES." I had passed, and I was now a Realtor.

OK, now what?

I had met a licensed realtor named Bryan Wilson at a disco where my girlfriend and I used to hang out. He told me that **anyone** would hire me – the question was, where did I want to work?

*Hmmm – so I get to choose, hey?* Yes. He told me to go interview three or four different Real Estate companies to get a feel for what they had to offer.

Well, you can imagine the surprise of some of these companies when a "green" 18-year-old made an appointment to interview them! I checked out an office in a small town where I grew up. They were happy to hire me if I wished, but I just kept thinking that I would only be seen as "little Penny Edgar", and wouldn't be taken seriously.

Off to the big city of Red Deer, Alberta. I interviewed one major company where the manager was found working down the street at a temp agency that he owned. *You'll never have time to train me,* I thought. Again, he would have hired me. *I'll keep looking,* I thought.

The office where Bryan himself worked was a very formal, very stiff environment. Everyone was made to wear suits, including the only lady who worked there.

The broker had me take a personality test. *I don't need any more tests,* I thought. Probably not a good fit for me.

Like Goldilocks, I soldiered on. I went over to Toole and Cote, the real estate agency where my best friend's mom, Henrietta, was a realtor. I interviewed Glen Buchwald, who gave me the straight goods:

**"Penny, you'll have to be twice as smart as anyone else to come across as half as good, because you are so young."** Right! Finally – someone telling me like it is!

He also offered to train me; plus, it was an office full of lovely ladies who I felt would take me under their wing and help me to learn the ropes. Sign me up![1]

The women in this office were like gods to me. I honestly thought that these women had psychic powers. We went on viewings together, which happened twice a week, and had us driving around the city to broker open houses, or just to check out all the new listings. As we drove by a house they would say, "That's a three bedroom, one bath, L-shaped living /dining room floor plan built by B&H homes." What? Did they see through walls? How could they know these things?

Would I be able to see through walls someday and know what was inside by merely looking at the exterior of a home?

Eventually, yes; I honed my superpowers over time, and can pretty well tell you what each home's floor plan is just by looking at the street and year of build – and maybe the colour of the carpet.

****

Having an energetic 18-year-old working for your company is like having a gerbil loose in the office.

On our open house excursions, I got a bit bored just going in and out of the buildings. At first, I thought I should take notes on each house so I could remember them. My clever colleagues assured me that I would get the hang of it without notes, and needn't rely on them. They were correct, so to keep myself entertained I would play little pranks instead. One day there was a stuffed cat on one of the beds, so I made meowing sounds (which I am quite good at, even cats think so). The other Realtors would jump up and think it was indeed a live animal, not stuffed.

There was one other Realtor in particular who would always leave his car running, and would rush in for a quick spin around the home. I would move his vehicle down the street to a different location from where he had originally parked; or turn the vehicle off, but first I would turn on the windshield wipers and crank the music – so when he turned it back on, all sorts of chaos would ensue! Tim was such a good sport and decided not to kill me off for this. He later became my manager and he was glad that he had let me live, as I turned out to be a top Realtor.

I would still get bored, however, and would try to convince my hard-working, stressed-out friends in the office to take a break for the afternoon and go to Sylvan Lake and drink beer. You could tell that these women really wanted to throw caution to the wind and head to the promise of a lake view and a cold beer, but they resisted (sigh).

---

[1] P.S. Alan Hodge – the slow exam writer – was now working at this agency, selling farms. He had a Grade 8 education, but boy, that old farmer knew his stuff. Shows you not to judge a book by what page he's on!.

I needed a project, obviously. *Where to find business?* One of my first clients was a you[ng] secretary who became a good friend – I even stood up at her wedding for her. She purchase[d a] tired mobile home for a few thousand dollars and transformed it into an adorable little hous[e] and was able to sell it for a profit. She may be the original house flipper. I think she was one [of] the only two people I have ever worked with that bought a trailer and made a profit.[2]

At this point, I had tapped into all the buyers in my office. No one else was going to buy a pla[ce] from me, as they were all Realtors too. I asked myself, "What can I do differently from wh[at] everybody else is doing so that I can make more money?"

What were most of them doing? They were sitting in the office, drinking coffee. Hmmm, well [I] didn't really like coffee, and would only use it as an emergency food supply – along w[ith] chocolate – to keep me going on a busy day. I figured if I cut out those two things (the sittin[g] and the coffee) there was a good chance I could earn more money.

So out the door I went, cards in hand, to chat with as many people as I could. My main goal [in] mind: to ask everyone I met if they wanted to buy or sell a house. I had heard a tip about takin[g] lunch in a busy mall and asking to sit with strangers because all the tables were full, so that[s] what I did. As I went about my days, every teller, grocery store clerk, curling club member, a[nd] gas station attendant got a card.

I quickly realized that by joining groups like the curling club, which I loved, I could make mo[re] connections; this is what we now call *networking*. I would just go curl, even seven days a we[ek] at one point. I bubbled over about all the fun things that were happening in real estate. I put [up] a big sign advertising my new status as a Realtor at the curling rink and, not long after, m[y] business began to grow. Word-of-mouth led from one sale to another, and I was off to the race[s].

Looking back over my career, it seems that the times I was having the most fun were also whe[n] I enjoyed the most success. So more play equals pay! Something to keep in mind – lately [it] seems it's all work and not much play.

What can I say? Even gerbils get caught up in the rat race.

---

[2] (Note to self: if there is no land attached the trailer is like a used car and it will depreciate. Land equal[s] increase in value).

"make the most money
get the quickest sale
and have the fewest
problems possible"

a  taught

# 2 THE ORIGINAL LIFE COACH

The tentative economy has everyone looking for direction - for someone to show them the way. If you choose wisely, life coaches may be worth their weight in gold.

Back in the 80's, my boss, Tim Moeler – who I had tortured earlier with moving his car around, etc. – told me about an upcoming event that he thought would change my career. He was right.

Before this, I had just been going along selling this or that and not really committing to real estate as a career. I wasn't selling a lot at the time – maybe because I didn't have the skills to feel as comfortable or as qualified as I wanted. I had even looked around to see about other work.

At Tim's urging, I signed up for the "List More, Sell More" sales event, led by Jerry Bresser – a very successful real estate trainer in Canada and the USA. Tim had attended one of his previous seminars and thought it would be a good fit for me.

I went to the introductory night and was surprised to find that this guru had all the answers to people's objections: from "go to HELL" to "I have a friend in the business" . He explained how I could net my clients more money than any other Realtor. They would have the best chance to **make the most money, get the quickest sale, and have the fewest problems possible.**

I had found the Holy Grail; the secret to my existence, the magic tools to make my clients' homes sell for more money – faster, and with fewer problems. No *logical* human could debate this method.

I coughed up a large sum of money to attend his three day course in Calgary. I rented a suite; it was only a few dollars more a night and offered a fireplace, double the space, and a giant conference table.

I invited Jerry over to chat at my swanky digs and he and I are still friends to this day. I listened carefully and took everything that he said very seriously. His course had cost a lot of money and I was going to get my money's worth! Every day we practiced and memorized language and techniques to help my sellers make good decisions that would net them more money.

Everyone else who was attending the course during the day hit the bar and visited at night – not me. I locked myself in my room and I talked to the walls as if they were my best clients: "There are eight good reasons why you will benefit by having me represent you to sell your home..."

Over and over like a master pianist, I practiced language, tone, and inflection until the words became my own. Jerry would say, "it's not a canned presentation; it's like the song, "Jingle Bells". Once a pianist has memorized it, he can improvise and add his own flair and expression, but the words are the same. I'm telling you, this one seminar changed the course of my career. My income doubled for quite a few years using these techniques.

For me, this was the best money I had ever spent. I went back at least three times and acquired my "Master Salesperson" designation, and continue to use what I learned there every day in my job.

I used to cringe when I would hear other agents telling their clients things like… they could price their home at whatever price they wanted, and if it didn't sell they could always drop the price later.

This is a terrible idea! You only get one chance to make a good first impression, so if it's overpriced to begin with, you've already lost most of your buyers.

Another thing they would say is that you don't have to prepare the home for showing, people have imagination, they can see past your clutter…. *uh, no they can't!* The closer it looks to a show home, the faster it will sell and for more money.

I could go on forever about the bad advice these Realtors were giving out. If they only knew the right answers, the right way to market, the right way to prepare a home for showing, to choose the best price and the best commission for their homes, they would be able to provide a more stress-free sale – for them, and for their clients.

As I always say to my clients, "if you can find someone who can get you more money, faster and with fewer problems, you should list with them; but I truly believe I am your best chance." This marketing program gave me the confidence to say that and mean it.

The training, education and techniques that I was able to master became my secret weapon. It gave me the information and solutions that I could relay to clients to help them net the most money possible, as quickly as possible and with the fewest problems possible.

Jerry's coaching was just what I needed to catapult my career. I was so *lucky* that Tim had encouraged me to attend.

# 3 DON'T PUT THE WOLF BEFORE THE PAYCHECK

I was 18 years old when I started in real estate (though the older I get, the younger I say I was when I started – yeah, I was actually 12, maybe 10... OK, I digress).

The point is, when you're that young and have an 'actual paying job' for the first time, you don't always make the best decisions with money.

Remember how I started out as Goldilocks, trying to find a company that was *just right*, and ended up working with a bunch of Mama Bears?

Well, now I was Red Riding Hood, venturing off on my own in the wild woods, knocking on doors and trying to drum up business.

It was very cold that year, and I was getting kidney infections from being outside all the time. One day, after being stood up by a client, I stopped in at a local furrier's to fill my time.

Mrs. Todd was an excellent saleslady, and had me try on a full-length wolf coat, in golds and browns and blacks – a prairie wolf's coat. It was so beautiful, and warm! I felt like a big teddy bear in it.

My client list was growing at this point, and though I had written quite a few offers lately, they all had conditions that needed to be met. Still, I did the math and thought that with all the offers rolling in I could surely afford this.

The coat cost $3000. At this time, minimum wage was $3.20 an hour – so in today's dollars the coat would have been about $14,000. I justified it by thinking I could now do more doorknocking, and make even more money. I took a leap, and purchased the coat.

However, I quickly discovered one small issue. The coat was so heavy that I couldn't walk very far in it, as the weight of it was too much. *"I'm not sure how those wolves do it,"* I thought.

Then another problem arose. Because I was so new to the business, I didn't realize that just because you had written an offer doesn't mean that the transaction is actually going to close, or that you're going to receive a paycheck. Every single deal that I had written fell through.

*OK, so now what am I gonna do?*

Well, thank goodness for awesome parents. My mom offered to cover half the cost of the coat for a Christmas/ birthday/ 'what a crazy daughter I have' present. Shortly after, I was able to earn the rest and pay off the balance I had placed on my credit card.

I still have the fur coat. Even though it appears to have shrunk ever so slightly, I still wear it – 40 years later – and it still looks like new. I wore it this evening to our office Christmas party, in fact, and I shared this very valuable lesson with some friends from the office: ***don't spend money you don't have yet.***

The wolf will wait!

"Tap into the
thing that
drives you"

a  thought

# 4 FAST CARS AND LIPSTICK

What motivates you? Rolex watches, Montblanc pens, feeding starving children, cars, bigger homes, travel, shoes…

Tap into the thing that drives you. Get a photo of whatever it is and paste it up on your wall.

Visualize it becoming a reality for you.

My first big goal in real estate was to get a Mercedes-Benz. A top Realtor came into our class at the real estate board one day, and I heard whispers all around the room of "he has a Mercedes".

That sounded like something I should get.

I called the Mercedes dealership in Calgary and asked them to send me a brochure and information on the 450 SL two-door convertible. The salesman sent me a black-and-white photocopy of the car. I put a tack in it and hung it up at my desk so that it would be front and centre every day, to remind me of what I was aiming for.

For my dream car, I decided on a baby blue one with grey interior. I had never seen that combination of colours on a car before, but I thought that those would be the colours for me.

I worked hard, and got to the point where I could get a loan for a car like that. It wasn't until I was 26 that I could go shopping for the vehicle I had been dreaming of since I was 18. That's a long time to wait!

At that point in my career, I could spend about $32,500 on the car. In those days, that was a lot of money! In today's dollars, I was spending $115,050. Yowza!

Before rushing straight to the closest Mercedes-Benz dealer, however, I went to many different dealerships, just to make sure there wasn't something that I would like more. At each one I was treated like a kid; a tire kicker. So, lesson number one in sales – never judge a book by its cover. I was probably the best qualified buyer that had been in that day, or maybe even that month.

One guy tried to sell me – as he referred to it – "the bottom of the line Saab". *Wow! That sounds sexy!* So I worked for years to qualify for this bottom-of-the-line car? No thanks!

I moved on. Most places didn't give me the time of day. Then I walked into Lone Star Mercedes and met Walter Floercke. Walter was a mature, German gentleman who clicked his heels together and saluted me and said, "If there's absolutely anything I can help you with, please don't hesitate to ask."

Now, there's a salesman!

In the showroom sat my dream car: the baby blue with grey interior, two-door convertible 450 S – the exact one I had been dreaming of. Wow, a manifested dream come true!

However, by that time I had realized that a two-door convertible wasn't really the best choice for a Realtor (or for Alberta winters). BUT the fact that it was there always astounded me.

I asked if I could drive one of the other cars in the showroom – a 190 E four-door model. I didn't know at that time that you couldn't actually test drive a brand new model. Instead, Walter took me on a test drive that I will never forget.

We went out and got into a "like-new" Mercedes. He drove first. We started out by burning donuts in a tight circle right there in front of all those brand new cars. I was a bit horrified that we might hit something, but we didn't. He wanted to show me the vehicle's tight turning radius. I was thrilled, and thoroughly impressed at this fun road test!

We headed out onto a bumpy washboard road and he showed me how it could stop and not chatter back-and-forth on the uneven surface. It just stopped smooth and in a straight line – so cool.

Now it was my turn. I got behind the wheel and he took me out onto the highway. We headed onto an overpass and Walter said, "Give it some gas!" I put the pedal down and *zoom* – we hit the curve in the road like a Lamborghini. I tell you, my smile was so big that if I had put lipstick on, it would've been on my ears!

Walter was impressed by my aggressive driving. He told me about driving at the Mercedes facility in Germany and that these cars could take a bank onto the track so their sides would be parallel to the ground as they went around the corner. Wow, that would be impressive to see.

So, I was sold – not on the two-door that I had originally dreamt of, but on the baby-blue four-door with a grey interior from the showroom, similar to the one that Walter and I had just taken for a ride.

I wasn't just going to give my money away, however. Some negotiation ensued, in which I told the manager of the company that I would be happy to pay an extra thousand dollars to buy a car from Walter as opposed to any other salesman that I had seen that day. I had a dollar amount in mind, and I ended up walking away from the purchase because we were $1500 apart.

Later, however, I got a call, and they said the regional manager had come in and said to go ahead and sell it to me at that price. Just because it was my dream car didn't mean I wasn't going to negotiate for the best price; what good is a car if you go bankrupt getting it?

*I learned a lot, buying this car. Firstly, that this goal setting or visualizing thing really works, and secondly, that I wanted to treat everyone, no matter their age or exterior, as if they were the most important client I've ever had.*

I had a similar experience later on with the new Mercedes SUV when it first came out in 1997. This time it was a burgundy model with a grey accent on the exterior that caught my attention. I had the colour brochure pinned up at my desk for 2 years, until my office moved to another building and the photo got packed away.

Some time later, I was at the Mercedes dealership looking at SUVs. I hadn't seen one I liked yet, and the prices were expensive. I asked if they might have one tucked away, perhaps a test model, lightly used, gently driven.

"Actually," said the salesman, "there is one..." and he took me into the back of the shop.

He showed me what turned out to be the boss' wife's car – she had custom-ordered a burgundy Mercedes with grey accents. Apparently, the only way that you could get this combination of colours was to custom-order it. It only had a few thousand kilometers on it and the price was right, so I bought it!

I had actually forgotten the exact colours of my dream vehicle until a while later, when I pulled out the brochure from the file that I had tucked away. There it was: the exact same car that was sitting in my driveway! How *lucky* was that?

*The mind is a powerful thing. Put it to good use, and it can help you achieve whatever it is that you were dreaming of.*

Trust me, it works better than you could ever imagine.

a  thought

"The mind is
a powerful thing.
Put it to good use,
and it can help you
achieve whatever it is
that you were dreaming of."

a thought

"It's not all sparkles and money"

# 5 REALTORS SHOULD GET HAZARD PAY

Many people think that working in real estate is a glamorous job.

On TV, the LA Realtors have diamonds, fast cars, and are selling mansions. Well, the real world is different…

I have had men try to take advantage of me on more than one occasion. I have had phone calls from potential buyers to the tune of, "Hey, can we try out the carpet when we check out that acreage?"

One year, most of the female Realtors in the office were receiving ongoing obscene phone calls, likely from the same creep. A lot of the ladies stopped doing open houses because this guy seemed to know where we all were, and we were all a little afraid. This was before the police could track people down by tracing phone calls.

Once, a friend of mine slipped on the ice showing houses. The listing Realtor had put the lockbox around the side of the house on the gas meter instead of on the front door, like most considerate Realtors do, and so my friend broke her hip on a patch of ice and was laid up for a very long time.

Another friend was viciously attacked by a dog when delivering flyers door to door. She had severe injuries that healed eventually, but emotionally, she never fully recovered.

One Realtor I know was showing a new house and the staircase collapsed, leaving several people injured. I stepped off a raised deck without a railing in the dark, breaking my ankle and leaving me unable to walk for 10 months.

I have had to go into houses where the walls were crawling with mould; there was no running water, and the filth in the kitchen and bathroom was so disgusting. The even sadder part was that the person living there had a skin disease from being in this horrid situation. I felt so bad for him.

I have had to clean an entire house before a showing, just to have a chance of selling it. After one such occasion, I even had a tenant complain because I had "touched his stuff." Excuse me, which stuff should I not have touched? The rag in the sink that smelled like a dead rat? The garbage bags stuck to the floor with Lord-knows-what seeping out of them? The five layers of crustiness on your stove? Should I not have thrown the comforter over your bed to hide the lovely black filth on your bare mattress?

Or maybe the food everywhere, or the empty takeout containers, or the dirt all over the floor? I told him that I had just wanted to help him out, as the person who was looking to buy the property had offered to keep him on as a tenant and I didn't want him to make a bad first impression. Oh… (lightbulb moment); and that's when he withdrew his complaint. Yes, how terrible of me to clean up your house *for free*.

I have had to show houses with dog poop on the floors, homes reeking of cat urine, containing active grow-ops or collapsing structures. Homes with giant lizards roaming free, snakes, tarantulas, vicious barking dogs, uncooperative angry tenants – you name it.

One house I evaluated was owned by a hoarder. The living room was so packed that I hadn't noticed her dog, and it was not a small dog, either. She owned a giant Husky, and he was sitting on her couch plain as day, but I literally could not see him for the piles of boxes, garbage and furniture that were everywhere. There were giant piles that she wanted me to climb over to see the bedrooms – "No that's OK, I know what a bedroom looks like". Lord only knows what was growing in the other rooms.

I've gotten stuck in the snow, and in sinking gravel driveways. I once drove my car onto land that was basically a swamp… I could have lost my new Mercedes.

I've had my drink spiked and escaped by the skin of my teeth from being raped.

So, ***it's not all sparkle and money***. Being a Realtor can be dangerous. None of us get paid as much as we should for some of the things that we have to endure.

But someone has to help these people sell their homes. They certainly aren't going to sell themselves!

# 6 BUCK NAKED BUYERS
# AND OTHER INDECENT PROPOSALS

Just before I started in real estate, I was out with friends at a bar one night. I met this older fellow, and we were talking about real estate. He was saying, "Oh, hey, you should come and look at this house that I have, and you can tell me what it's worth."

It was out of town, in a centre close to Red Deer. I said, "well, you know, I don't really know anything about anything", and tried to talk him out of it. But, he just kept insisting that I should really come by; that it would be good practice for me.

So, as naive as I was, I went along. He drove me to this vacant house in a small town, and proceeded to follow me around as I inspected the house. Eventually, it came to light that he thought he should have his way with me.

Well, that's when I began my sales career, right then and there. I was talking my way out of the situation; negotiating him out of trying to accost me.

I managed to persuade him out of it, and we got back in the car to drive back to Red Deer. I was thinking *phewf, I made it; I talked my way out of that one*. He then informed me that he was going to show me an acreage that he owns, so maybe I could list it sometime and sell it. It was beginning to seem like I didn't really have any choice in the matter. So he took me out to this vacant field, in the middle of I-still-don't-know-where, and tried to do it all over again.

Again, somehow, using my lovely sales skills that I was quickly acquiring, I convinced him that if he just took me back I wouldn't tell anybody what had happened. I wouldn't tell them who he was, as nothing had happened. Somehow, he managed to believe me and took me back.

That was not the only indecent proposal that I have had in my career.

One time, I went over to do an evaluation on a young man's house, and afterwards he said, "Okay, so you should have sex with me and then I'll give you the listing." *Um, what?!* He said, "Well, the other lady that did the evaluation said she would." (*Sure, she did!) Well, I guess then she can have the listing*!

There was also an older gentleman who thought that he should get to kiss me because he bought a house. *Yeah, no, that's not the way it works.*

So there's a lot of really interesting things that people think they should get in exchange for doing business but *this girl does not have sex for listings.*

During my first year in real estate, I worked at an office mainly made up of ladies. One day, a man phoned and said he wanted to go look at houses. I volunteered to show him around.

I still remember driving up to this house. It was a half-duplex. As I was walking up I was thinking *wow, this is a really tall fence*. It was a six-foot cedar fence. I'd never seen a fence that tall.

I opened the big gate. Straight ahead of me was a guy lying buck naked on his lawn chair, in all his glory. And I'm thinking, *Oh my word!* I turned back around towards the gate and said I was the Realtor here to show him around, and was he ready to go?

He could see how awkward I felt. He grabbed a teeny face cloth and placed it over his genitals as he was talking to me. Eventually, we went into the house. Why did I go into the house? I don't know.

I said, "You know, you should probably get dressed", to which he replied, "Oh, are you embarrassed by people without clothes?" *Well, yeah.* Red Deer may be known for many things, but a large quantity of nudist colonies is not one of them.

"On second thought," I said, "I don't think I want to show you any houses today." I left and went back to the office.

I walked in, eyes like a deer caught in headlights, and they all burst out laughing. I guess this was not the first time that this 'gentleman' had done that to a Realtor; a few of them had already experienced the same thing. I didn't actually think it was as funny as they did, but they got quite a kick out of it.

Needless to say, I don't really like working with naked buyers. Just not my forte'.

When I think back on these things now, I think, *Wow, if I could talk myself out of being raped or having to have sex with people or having to deal with naked buyers, I could probably do pretty well in this job. If I were quick on my feet and calm in my speech, I could sell a lot of houses and convince people of good things that would help them.*

Little did I know that I was honing my sales skills in a way that most people really wouldn't take a class in. It was a lesson in survival and negotiation and selling skills.

**The Art of Counter-Seduction 101: Clothes on, pencils up, everyone!**

"Paying it forward absolutely pays off!"

a thought

# 7 BREAK AND ENTER
# AND OTHER ACTS OF KINDNESS

Giving back is a way of life for me. I am usually sensitive to the needs of others and at Christmastime, even more so.

One of my favorite things to do with my kids when they were younger was what we called 'Ring and Run'. We would find people who were having a tough year, and try to make their Christmas a little more cheerful.

We would drive close to their house, and carry the boxes quietly to the door. I would drive down the street a bit and the boys would knock like crazy and then run, run, run for all they were worth. They would jump in the car and we would drive off like bandits – go go go!

We didn't want to get caught; the point was to give, without any thanks necessary. No takebacks!

One year, we found out about a family that didn't have a TV, so we actually broke into the house through an open patio door and left a TV and other gifts. Break in and leave, instead of break in and steal. Not exactly legal, but no one complained.

Another year, we took stacks of money and the boys went around the mall giving money away to moms with kids. It was the best thing to see the boys spread Christmas joy to total strangers.

We would ask at schools or friends to see if they knew of anyone in need. We would bring all the fixings for turkey dinner: potatoes, stuffing, gravy, vegetables, buns, you name it – plus dessert. One year, someone had placed an ad on Kijiji saying that they didn't have enough money for a Christmas tree. We gave them more than the tree. We sprung for a Christmas dinner and presents, and a tree with decorations.

One such drop-and-run was for one of my favourite clients. She was a single mom with awesome kids. They lived on very little and I could never figure out how she made ends meet, but she did, while being so generous to others. I wanted to give her an extra boost to lift her spirits. I loved hearing about how excited the kids were to receive the gifts and extra bounty.

I tell you these stories not to brag – instead, I want to encourage you to try it. Giving is seriously addictive. Give it a try; you will love it! I truly believe the verse "it is better to give than receive". ***Paying it forward absolutely pays off!***

I am often asked why my kids are so great.

The answer: two moms and a hovercraft dad. Having the kids constantly close is one reason they've become the wonderful people they are.

Darlene homeschooled the boys. One of the things we learned through homeschooling was that if children are associated with people of different ages, especially adults, they tend to act more mature. Our boys developed many long lasting friendships with their peer groups, became defenders of the young, and were able to interact well with adults, too.

I also told them that teenagers weren't allowed in the house, meaning that they were boys, and then they were young men; but never "teenagers". I love teenagers, but I wanted my boys to skip over some of the pressures of being a stereotypical teenager and just be men – strong and confident.

One way to keep an eye on them in their teen years: be the house where all the kids want to be.

We had so many kids come through our home – we fed them so much pizza, waffles, eggs, and bacon that we should have opened our own diner.

We were "the fun house". Poker games, sleepovers, fire pits, epic Nerf wars, Dungeons & Dragons, Xbox LAN parties. We even would take extra kids on holiday with us. We loved it and still consider many kids that are friends with our boys to be "our kids".

One of my better parenting ideas was to bribe Bryce. He was turning 18, and going after his real estate license. I sat him down, and offered him $5000 if he wouldn't drink until he was 21.

I did this for two (mostly selfish) reasons:

1. I wouldn't have to worry about the trouble that he might get into by drinking. I had been there, done that, and it wasn't pretty. If he could avoid those pitfalls, all the better.

2. If I needed him to go and show a house or drive a client somewhere, he would not be impaired and would be available to work whenever needed.

It took a few days for him to think over my proposal. *Luckily,* he said he would accept the terms of my offer. And he followed through, right up to the big payout on his 21st birthday.

It worked out well for both of us: I knew he was safe as far as sobriety was concerned, and he was earning quite a bit from our joint real estate ventures, with the promise of the $5000 ahead of him.

The money proved a useful tool for when his friends would try and get him to drink. "Oh I can't," he'd say. "Why not?" they would ask. "Well, if I did it would cost me $5000," he'd explain, pointing out exactly how much he stood to lose and why. Instead of continuing to pressure him, his friends would inevitably say, "Boy, I wish my mom and dad would have done that for me!"

Wouldn't you pay to know that your child was safe? It may be the best money you'll ever spend! It actually worked out great for all of his friends, too, as he ended up being the designated driver on many occasions. So not only was he safe, but he was keeping all his friends out of danger, too.

Stay close to your kids. Be the house where they and their friends want to hang out.

**Love them fiercely, and bribe them if necessary.**

"Live now, travel now; do all the things you're passionate about!"

# 9 AHEAD OF THE CURVE

When I was 33, I purchased a condo in Kona on the Big Island of Hawaii. It was a beautiful top-floor unit at the Surf and Racquet Club.

My youngest son, Bryce, was about two years old at the time we bought the place. He was a pretty quiet kid, and though he and his brother Cole would play in the condo, they weren't really making any more noise than anyone else. Still, the cranky downstairs neighbor would yell up at us to "keep it down". One time, I piped back that they were just kids, and weren't doing anything wrong.

A while later, there was a knock at the door. I opened it to find the resident manager standing there – he had received a noise complaint. He said "I'm not sure who rented you this unit seeing that you have kids, but they shouldn't have."

"I own it," I replied, to which he stammered something to the tune of, "Oh … well … ahh. The people downstairs are just complainers," after realizing he was now offending me, an owner.

I did feel a bit badly later about having possibly disturbed the other residents, and it was almost Valentine's Day, so I took Bryce by the hand, soother, tousled curly hair and all, down to their unit and knocked on the door.

The neighbours opened up to Bryce in all his cuteness who said, "I'm torry for making noise", and handed them some chocolates. The formerly cranky neighbour moved down to one knee to be at his eye level and said, "Oh, that's OK honey – it's not your fault, you weren't doing anything wrong!"

My age, combined with those of my kids, was a lot younger than most of the other holidayers in the condo building but that didn't stop us. I decided years ago that I wanted to live like I was retired – all the fun parts that it is – like traveling to warm places for extended periods of time, exploring Europe and vacationing in the mountains and at the lake. I wasn't going to wait until I got old, because you never know how long you have on this earth. I decided I didn't want to miss out on any of it, just in case I don't get the chance when I'm retired.

People say that when you retire you should start living it up. I want to live it up now. My advice to you is to **live now, travel now; do the things you're passionate about.** You don't have to wait, just plan, focus and do it! Don't be 'torry – live your life!

# 10 BITCOIN, SWEAT, TREES, AND OTHER FORMS OF CURRENCY

People talk about creative financing as if it was something new. I was doing rent-to-owns before they were cool.

I've carried financing in the form of second mortgages. I even had an 82-year-old lady carry a first mortgage once. You may think that was a bit crazy, but I had a good solid buyer that just needed a year or so before they could qualify, so I put the idea to my client about carrying the mortgage until the newcomers could take it over. She said "That would be perfect; my son will get most of the money from the sale of the home, so this way he can't spend it all at once – he can only spend a little bit each month." Plus, she made way more because of the extra interest she earned carrying the financing, rather than just putting her cash in the bank.

Back in 2013, I offered to sell an acreage that I owned for Bitcoin. The *National Post* picked up the story: "Alberta woman willing to trade $1 million property for bitcoin – the volatile new digital currency". The funny thing was that a week before, I hadn't even known what bitcoin was – my son, Cole, had told me a little about it and said, "Hey Mom, you should offer your house for sale for bitcoin" and I said, "Sure honey, what's that?"

The article went viral – it was translated into at least five languages. We still get interesting phone calls from different newspapers and writers around the world asking questions about bitcoin.[3] As I say in the article, I'm interested in taking things on trade. I'll even take chickens on trade.

I am also a fan of sweat equity – doing work on your own home to increase the value of your property, or even turning some of your 'sweatbucks' into part of a down payment. At one point, we purchased an acreage outside of Bowden, and we worked on remodeling it using sweat equity, keeping the wage the contractor would have earned. In the end, we only had to put $1500 cash of our own money into the purchase because we had been able to increase the value of the property by so much that when we turned around to get the mortgage in place, we had already financed out 98% of the value of the house.

One of the best ideas I ever had came to me when I was working for a client looking to buy a quarter section – 160 acres of land – with a trailer and a huge shop on it. They only needed an extra $30,000 to have enough for the down payment.

---

[3] Fun fact: they talked about this being a volatile currency, but when we were considering selling the place for bitcoin, the average bitcoin was worth $1257. Today, it's worth $9570. If I had taken the bitcoin and hung onto it, I would have made $7,613,000. Even if I had cashed it all in except for $50,000 in bitcoin, it would now be worth $380,000, so I would have sold the property, in essence, for $1.330 million. I guess I wasn't so crazy after all.

Hmmm... as I pondered what to do, I looked around at this beautiful piece of property that was about 70% covered with giant spruce and Tamarack trees. I remembered reading about a small logging company with mules that would do "selective logging". This means that they would go in and choose trees and cut them down, and then they would, very carefully with as little disturbance as possible, bring the logs out of the forest.

The best part was that I had calculated that each tree was worth approximately $1000, so all we needed was 30 trees. The new owners wouldn't even miss these trees with all the forest cover that remained. We approached the sellers to carry financing for a few weeks until we could log the trees with their permission.

It all worked out: the purchasers put together the money that they needed from the sale of the trees, and they were able to go to the bank and put a mortgage in place to buy the property. They – and their kids – are now some of my most faithful clients.

Sometimes **you have to "see the trees for the forest!" I like getting creative and thinking outside the box – creating a win-win for everyone!**

 a  thought

"Life will throw you curveballs.
Grab them and throw them right back!"

# 11 DOG SH#T STORY

*"People want what you have, but they don't want to do what you had to do to get it".*
— *Darlene Kander*

Many people would love to have an oceanfront condo in Hawaii, a cabin at the lake, a few investment properties, and a nice home – but when I tell people what I had to do to get them, they aren't so keen to jump in and take action.

When I started buying houses, I would have to subsidize each place by an average of $300 a month. I'll give you an idea of what that cost me. At that time, the average person worked for $3.25 an hour; so if I'd had a regular job, I would have had to work 94 extra hours a month to pay for the privilege of owning one extra house. I did it gladly, as I knew the benefits of owning real estate and building wealth. At least that's what I hoped.

Nowadays, if I show a client a suited house, they would want to earn $500 a month cash flow as their income after paying out all expenses. If I had waited for that, I would never have owned anything. It just wasn't something that you could do back then; at least, I never found any way to do it. Sometimes, even when I do find a house that fits their criteria, the client still doesn't want to buy it.

OK folks, it's your choice, but if you don't have any risk you won't have any reward.

It's not always rewarding. Just like prices, risk goes up and down with the market. When I was a single mom with two kids, I had five of my tenants decide all in the same month not to pay me the rent. I remember knocking on the door of a tenant with a baby on my hip, trying to get them to pay the rent. "Nope, we used it for a down payment on a house". And then they slammed the door.

*OK, so now what?* I wasn't about to ruin my credit by not making these five mortgage payments, but what could I do? What could I sell? All I really had that I could liquidate quickly was my vehicle. A lovely blue Trooper SUV.

A short time later, I was walking down the main street and I bumped into one of my favorite clients, and we got to chatting. I asked him if he might be interested in purchasing a vehicle, and he said "as a matter of fact, I am".

He had just been renting a car for the last few months and was looking to own. I had bought the Trooper at a good price and had driven it for 10 months. I was able to sell it to him for about what I had initially paid. So, in a way, I drove the car for 10 months for free. That was *lucky!*

I took the money and made my mortgage payments on time, but I was now without a vehicle Tricky being a Realtor with no car! Sometimes I borrowed my nanny's car, but when she had enough of that I took a taxi to my parents' farm and borrowed their car for a short time Eventually, I saved up my money and paid cash for a cool old 1978 Mercedes 450 SL – it was only $8000, but it looked like a million bucks. I think people were more impressed with that car than with the more expensive ones I've owned since.

Over the span of my career, I have seen properties go up $100,000 in one year and drop $50,000 in another. I have been so strapped that I had no credit left, no money in the bank and I could hardly buy a cup of coffee. I have been real estate rich, but cash poor. I have bartered to pay the babysitter and borrowed money from my own kids and parents to keep going. I have had lots of hours of worry and frustration over bad tenants and things that needed fixing, like leaky roofs and exploding hot water tanks. I have fixed my rental while my own house had to wait because I had to keep the tenants happy.

The sad part is, although I sacrificed much for my tenants, they often felt entitled and acted like I had all the money in the world just because I owned more than one house. I wish tenants truly realized the investment of time, money and energy that goes into the homes they are lucky enough to rent. No stress on their side, just a great place to live, and if something breaks or goes wrong they just have to pick up the phone and magically it's all fixed (at least with good landlords that is; and that's what I tried to be).

Do I sound disgruntled? Well, maybe a little sometimes. I guess I make it look easy. Bryce asked me one day, *if I could do something over in my life, what would it be*? I said,"I would have more kids and I would buy more houses."

What can I say, **some girls buy shoes, I buy houses.**

Maybe I should have played it safe and purchased shoes and scarves instead of 4-plexes and condos. Oh, but then there would be no home in Hawaii, or cabin at the lake. It's difficult to earn your way to these things with a typical day job – you need the leverage that real estate provides. Where else can you invest $14,000 (which was 20% of a house that I had bought for $70,000) and have it go up by $100,000 in less than two years, only to sell it, making over seven times the original investment? **Sounds easy, you should do it. Or should you?**

**Wait for it...**
This particular investment is one of my favorite landlord stories of all time. I often refer to it as the "*dog sh#t story*".

I had rented out a house built in the early 1900's to a cool couple; they were tattooed and pierced and life was grand. They paid their rent on time, they renovated the house for me; while I just had to pay for a few building materials, they did all the labour.

Everything was good until they went into business for themselves, lost everything, and turned to drugs for comfort. They stopped paying the rent. They had four Rottweilers that they would leave in the house unattended. By the time I was ready to call the SPCA on them for cruelty to animals, these dogs had scratched, chewed and sh#t their way through the entire house - walls, doors and door frames – you name it! It was the worst disaster I have ever seen. To make matters worse, my sons were partners with me in this real estate venture as I had been putting away all their baby bonuses instead of spending them. I had put it in mutual funds and cashed them in to help put part of the down payment on this property.

Well, no time like the present for a life lesson on being a landlord. I said to my boys, "if you're going to be a landlord, you need to see how bad it can get." I took them both with me; they were about 13 and 17 at the time. We started by shoveling the sh#t that filled the house into a large four-foot metal box that the tenants had left behind. As if that wasn't disgusting enough, when we went to load the box into the truck we realized that there were holes in it and the poop was leaking out, leaving a trail of crap everywhere!

When we got to the dump, it smelled so bad they would not let us dump into the main area where everyone else was dropping off their trash. Instead, they made us drive out to the back of the property, where we drove up to the very top of a giant mountain of trash and offloaded it there. I don't even think it was safe to be driving across this mountain of refuse.

I didn't make the boys do any more of the cleaning on this property. A fellow that I hired helped me to finish it up. I had already sold the house to the neighbours, who had agreed to accept the property as is, even knowing how bad it was but I couldn't in good conscience leave the place in that disgusting condition. I cleaned it all up before turning it over to them.

Would you be willing to shovel tons of dog crap to get a condo in Hawaii? I think most people would say no.

*Real estate investing is rewarding in the long run, but it's not for the faint of heart.*

"Some girls buy shoes,
I buy houses."

# 12 MISPLACED AT BIRTH

When I was 14 years old, my Grandpa Edgar took my brother and I to Hawaii on a trip. He did this with each grandchild when they reached the age of 14. He had been to Hawaii for 50 years in a row and owned an apartment at the *Rosalie* building in the very first high-rise in Waikiki.

I still remember to this day the moment that I got off the plane and the humidity and the warmth hit me like a wave. It had been -30F when we left Calgary. My grandfather was still wearing his long underwear when we arrived in Hawaii, and he was sweating profusely.

The moment I felt Hawaiian air, and smelled the wonderful fragrance of the trees and the flowers, my first thought was: *I was misplaced at birth – I should live here.*

Since then, I have been to the Hawaiian Islands approximately 40 times in my life. I haven't gotten tired of it yet, and it is hard for me to leave the island each time I have to return to Canada.

One of my favorite things that I ever bought was a condo in Hawaii when I was in my early 30's. Bryce was only two years old, and I was nowhere near retirement. In retrospect, I bought it about 20 years ahead of schedule. I wasn't really in a position to spend a lot of time there yet, because of the kids' school and shared visitation.

I bought this condo with $30,000 down and had the owner carry a mortgage at 4% for 10 years because it's difficult to get financing in the States as a Canadian. We are seen as a risk. Maybe it's because they can't come after us if we don't pay as easily as if we lived in the United States. So I only owned it for a couple of years, because owning a quarter of a million dollar condo and only getting to live there for 10 days out of a year and having to rent it out the rest of the time wasn't any fun. After a while, I sold it; it was one of the few things that I actually lost money on.[4]

Through the years, I kept my eye on the market. Every time I would go to Hawaii, I would do research. Fifteen years later, I was in a little art and accessory store on Kauai and I found a little coin that says, **If not now, when?** I began thinking, *you know, I think it's time. I think it's time to buy something if I can find something.*

We found this wonderful pair of awesome Realtors, Ruthie and her husband, Don Schultz. We were looking to get a two bedroom, two bath – that's all we wanted to buy. But as Ruthie was showing us houses said, "oh, I have to go do an open house now, and you should come over and look at it." Well, *an open house is like crack to me.* I will go look at open houses all day long. I know it's my job, but that's also what I like to do for fun. So we went to look at this condo.

---

[4] Now that Airbnb exists I probably could have kept it and done very well and may not have had to sell it. Again, I was ahead of the times.

It was the end unit, second floor, away from the parking lot, and right next to a beautiful, lush ravine. We walked in the door, and **BAM!**: ocean everywhere – ocean on the side, ocean at the front, even when you're on the back master bedroom lanai[5] because of the way it was situated. It was only a one-bedroom but it was huge, about 960 square feet. It had two bathrooms (the two bathrooms were actually more important than the two bedrooms, because they had a pull-out couch in the living room, too). I'm like, *done. We are buying this!*

So, I actually ended up putting offers on two properties that year; this one, and another less expensive one I had looked at first. I talked to my bank and my mortgage broker said "yeah, you can swing two". I was already of the mindset that **you should take two, they're small**, so this was music to my ears.

We ended up letting the one on the ocean go... at first. I was being sensible and I was going to buy only the more affordable one at $200,000 and have money left over to do a renovation. I spoke to the kids on the phone about it. They said that seemed like the sensible thing. It was a two bedroom, two bath, noisier location, not as good of a building, but you know, what are you going to do?

The kids came over to Kauai for a holiday, and I said, "well, let's just drive by. I'll show you the one that I let go." Cole walked around the front of the building, and was wowed by the oceanfront, a 100 foot cliff, ocean as far as the eye can see. He said, "Mom, wouldn't you rather have this one?" *Well, yeah.* He said, "even if we have to lend you the money, you should get this one." So we let the 2nd one go because the broker was unable in the end to secure financing for two places. Too bad; I would still love to have 2, because 2 are always better than one.

I went on to arrange financing for the property in a really creative way: I borrowed against my own inheritance. My dad had a large life insurance policy with a cash value that will eventually become partly my inheritance so he phoned and suggested that we borrow against that. So, I basically borrowed my inheritance to buy this condo, and enjoy what I believe should have been my birthright – living in beautiful Hawaii. My dad loved Hawaii and he was so thrilled to see me enjoying this dream and he and mom even stayed there a bit too. What parent wouldn't want to see their kids enjoy their inheritance now, rather than waiting for them to pass away first?

We continue to go every year, if possible, to stay in our Hawaiian home. So even though I can't live there year-round like the islander I wish to be, I am so **lucky** to get to enjoy it for a few months each year; and for now that will have to do.

A roofed, open-sided porch or balcony originally from Hawaii.

# 13 YOU CAN'T MAKE THIS SH#T UP

Where do I start...

Well, it was September 2007. I was showing an acreage for a fellow Realtor who was on holiday. The clients had looked at the property for hours. I had let them know that they were welcome to take as long as they wanted, but we ended up being there so long that the sun had firmly set before they headed home to contemplate the purchase.

I went around the house and turned off all the lights, because clients get really cranky if lights are left on after a showing. It was pitch black out there in the country. I headed out of the house the back way, towards where I had parked the car. I was thinking as I was walking that this must be a ground level deck as there were no railings. So I stepped off into the dark void, but there was no immediate ground there to catch me. On the way down, my foot caught between two large boulders and my ankle went over sideways.

I fell flat on my face. My cell phone, lockbox key and real estate folder went flying in every direction. I immediately felt the pain and knew that I was in trouble. I groped around in the dark, trying to locate my phone and lockbox key. I found my phone first, but this was years before they had any trusty flashlight features. Somehow, I managed to find all my stuff, but when I tried to stand up... *yeah, that was not going to happen*. There was no way I could bear weight on my right foot.

I hopped/dragged myself over to the shiny new Mercedes I had just purchased the month before. I could feel my ankle swelling, and was in so much pain I felt nauseated – I thought I might faint. I managed to get into the vehicle and phone Darlene to let her know what had happened. I told her I was going to try and get home and if I didn't make it in a half hour, I had probably passed out in the ditch somewhere.

I don't know if you've ever tried to drive with your left foot, but it doesn't work so well. I used stick control and clicked the up-and-down feature on the steering wheel to increase my speed, which worked fine until I got to a corner. I tried to brake, and it was like trying to pet a budgie with a sledgehammer. My foot went down too hard and I was in danger of throwing myself through the windshield.

I managed to make it the half hour home, and crawled up the stairs to my room. This was late on a Saturday night, and I decided that even though the pain was unbearable, the thought of sitting in the ER for hours on a "party night" was more distasteful. I told Darlene that if I felt like I needed to go to the hospital I would let her know. Well, it was a restless night to say the least. I woke up at 6 a.m. and called her to say that I really needed to go to the hospital. It was quite a while before she came upstairs to get me and at this point, tears were rolling down my face. "Oh dear, I had no idea you were in that much pain!" she said.

We went to Emergency in the quiet morning hours and had almost no wait time. I sat in the room waiting for the doctor. He walked in and took one look at me, as I was sitting there with tears streaming down my face.

He then asked the strangest question: "Have you ever given birth to a child?" *Huh? Do you have my chart mixed up with somebody else's? Why are you asking me this weird question?* I said, "Yes, two natural deliveries, with basically no drugs. Why do you ask?" "Well, now I know how much pain you're in," he said. *Okay, so not the craziest question after all.*

He sent me for an x-ray and when it came back, said he believed it to be a bad sprain. My foot was swollen and purple and green and the size of a giant squash. "Get a boot – a large one – and stay off it for six weeks," he said. *Um, what?* This had been one of the busiest, if not the busiest, year I had ever seen. I was the only breadwinner, and now I was laid up and unable to walk.

Weeks went by without any improvement, so finally I went back to see my GP, who reviewed the x-ray. "Hmm, looks like it may be broken," he said. *You think!*

More x-rays confirmed that I had crushed my talus – the main bone that helps you stand. Surgery was set for March, 6 months away! I couldn't wait that long; I needed to walk. I had already paid for a CT to confirm what was broken, but now I needed surgery.

I asked my orthopod if there was a faster way, and he told me that I could pay for surgery with a specialist, rather than waiting in line. I did some googling, and found a clinic in Vancouver that looked promising, run by a Dr. Alistair Younger. I mentioned all this to my doctor, who looked at me, eyes wide, and said that Dr. Younger was probably the best in his field in Canada, and that he was personally lucky enough to have studied under him. *Well, why didn't you mention that in the first place!*

Fast forward to a few weeks later: Bryce, Darlene and I flew to Vancouver. We upgraded to a suite on the top floor of our hotel so that I would have more space to recover. The morning of the surgery, Darlene 'borrowed' the hotel wheelchair and wheeled me the block or so to the clinic for my surgery.

Charming, professional doctors greeted me one by one. Thinking I was some kind of thrillseeker or *Grey's Anatomy* junkie. They asked if I wanted to be awake for the surgery. *Hell no, thank you, just go ahead and put me under.* I awoke sometime later, very loopy and full of jokes.

Dr. Younger informed me that it was much worse than they had initially thought. When he went in with his scopes and tools, the bone literally disintegrated as they tried to remove what they had thought was just a bone fragment. It was a teaching hospital, so I was able to get a video copy of the procedure. The little grabber-like Pac-Man character just kept taking bites of the bone, and it came away as easily as eating cottage cheese. Two thirds of my talus had disappeared. He wasn't sure how it would go with walking, but he had a positive outlook. We went back home, where I was violently ill from the wonderful painkillers the hospital had provided. I went off of those immediately, and took Advil or Tylenol instead for the next several years – yup, I said years. Before this, I had never even touched aspirin.

I was unable to walk and I developed what was called RSD, now called Complex Regional Pain Syndrome, which made my leg turn purple all the way up and caused the nerves to be hypersensitive. Even a blanket touching my foot at night was excruciating. When my foot was not elevated, the pain was unbearable. Most days I sat with an ice pack on it all day. I sat with ice on my foot for weeks and weeks. If it wasn't for that ice I don't think I would have made it; I may have gone crazy.

Despite the pain and lack of insurance after surgery, I decided to take my annual trip to Kauai. The 'pain ride,' as I refer to it, was the longest plane ride of my life. Eight hours, but it felt like a hundred. I was supposed to get a seat with an extra amount of legroom at the front, but that didn't happen, and the flight attendant, who seemed to think I was faking, kept hitting my leg every time she walked by. It was horrible!

I went to the doctor as instructed when I arrived to get a prescription for physiotherapy. I took all my x-rays with me. The nurse practitioner took my info and scans and consulted with the doctor for quite a while. When she came back in, she looked a little grey. She stammered and said that the doctor had reviewed my records and concluded that with an injury as severe as mine, I would never walk on the ankle again. Furthermore, I needed to go immediately to New York and get a full ankle replacement. *Oh no, thank you, I'll be fine; I'm not leaving my Hawaiian holiday. Forgo the sun and warmth and tropical heaven for a hospital in New York? Forget it!* I got my physio prescription and left.

The best part of rehabbing in Hawaii was when my stitches had finally healed, and I could get into the pool and float around. It was the only time I felt human. Weightless, effortlessly floating with the pool noodle. I never wanted to get out.

We had to trade our second-floor condo with the ocean view for a ground-floor unit, as that was the only way I could get in and out of the building. I wasn't able to look at places that I loved because I couldn't get down to the beach; the effort was too much for me to walk through the sand with crutches. Ultimately, I didn't mind any of it; I was in Hawaii, my happy place. After five blissful weeks, I headed home.

No money was coming in, so I had to work. I remember the first day I hobbled around to show houses. I had to have my boys drive me to showings, as I certainly couldn't drive myself. The first house I showed was vacant and there was nowhere for me to sit. I was in tremendous pain, the client was late arriving and I was just about going crazy and wanted to cry and go home but that wasn't an option. I persevered. The kids would take me to showings, and I would sit in the entryway and they would tour the clients around.

One client who wanted to buy a nice suited property I had listed kept countering every offer my seller would make. I would crutch it into the back room, talk to the seller, come back out and he would just keep countering. It got to the point where I was in so much pain that I said I would take no commission just so he could have it, and I could go home. He said, "Hm, I'll think about it." I went home and collapsed on the couch.

The next day, a full price offer came in from an out-of-town buyer who had seen what a good deal it was over the Internet. Sold! Sure enough, a few hours later, the buyer I had been negotiating with the previous day called me and said he had decided to go ahead with the deal that we had discussed. "Sorry," I said, "that ship has sailed."    He said, "But that was a really good deal," and I said, "Yeah, I told you that yesterday." He actually kept phoning back every few days still trying to negotiate. *Nope – you snooze you lose. You only get so many chances.*

Ten months later, it was just before my birthday and my mom was giving me her thoughts on my extremely painful leg. She had read about a lady that had her leg cut off and replaced with a prosthetic, and about how great she was doing. She thought maybe that was something I should look into. I said, "Mom, I'd rather live in a wheelchair the rest of my life than cut off my leg." At that point I told God, "You know God, I haven't really asked you for anything this year. It's my birthday, and I want to walk."

On June 14, 2008, my birthday, I threw my crutches away, replaced them with two canes and started walking. It was very painful, but I refused to go back to the crutches.

For the next seven years I suffered from RSD, unable to stand for any amount of time, and in constant pain. I tried drugs recommended by my pharmacist cousin to block the nerve pain, but it barely took the edge off. I eventually got better, but even today I still can't stand in line for long periods of time, especially on concrete, but at least I have my leg — *which I am extremely attached to; in more ways than one!* 😊

Later on, in 2014, when I was finally feeling some relief from the nerve pain in my right leg, I found this lump on my left knee and no one seemed to know what it was. I went to the doctor in September. He was pretty sure it was a lipoma, or in layman's terms, a lump of fat – 99.99% of the time they were just benign fatty tissue. So I went home, but the pain kept increasing, so I went back at the end of December, just before I was supposed to fly to Hawaii. "It really hurts when I lie on it," I said, and they agreed to do an ultrasound.

The call came in after the results of the ultrasound reached my doctor. "You need to come in to see the doctor right away." It's never good when the doctor's office calls and tells you that you need to come in right away. Dr. Stearn, my kind, caring physician, explained that I had the other

.01% – which is cancer, a type called Sarcoma. He explained that Sarcoma is so rare that in all the time that he had worked in hospitals he had never seen one, until now. *Lucky me.*

He shared, "yesterday I had to tell a young father of three that he had cancer." He said that he was so sad when he got home that he went into his office, put on his headphones to listen to music and told his wife he wanted to be alone. He said, "Now, I just want to go home and cry." Poor guy! He took it worse than I did. I told him not to worry and that I was going to be fine. Yep; me, ever the optimist.

On January 12, we went down to Calgary and stayed at a hotel close to the hospital where I would get a biopsy the next day to confirm the suspicion of sarcoma. We left 45 minutes early for a five minute drive. Only one problem: there was no place to park. We drove around the parkade five times with no luck. I told Darlene I would just get out and go so as not to miss the doctor, as he was fast-tracking my appointment and my biopsy was scheduled between two of his surgeries.

I was up there in the waiting room for some time... no Darlene. Where was she? Then, I got a text: *I've fallen and I think I've broken my leg.*

Really? Today you're going to punk me, seriously? But sure enough, a few minutes later, two very shaken workmen entered with Darlene in a wheelchair. One of them explained. "She fell, she went down and I'm sure she broke her leg!" He was so rattled, and what did I do? I laughed. I'm thinking, *you can't make this sh#t up. Really, of all the days, today you break your leg? Of course, today!*

The people in the waiting room must have thought I was on drugs. My poor wife had broken her leg and I was laughing. We went up to the desk again to explain what had happened. We would have had to take her to emergency for triage if the workmen hadn't seen her go down. They were on the other side of the glass by the elevator and saw as Darlene had rushed to come in, hitting a curb which acted like a fulcrum, and down she went. The receptionist said she would talk to the doctor.

Enter Dr. Monument: a very tall, handsome doctor: sparkly eyes, big grin, kind heart! Also turns out he is a rockstar in his field! *I hit the "lucky" jackpot!!*

He said he assumed Darlene was the patient who needed the biopsy, as she was in a wheelchair and I was walking. We explained that she had broken her leg twenty minutes before. He rubbed his hands together and with a grin of anticipation said, "don't drink anything, just in case we get to do surgery. I'll just get permission from your doctor to treat you like a referral."

Moments later, Dr. Stearn phoned out of the blue to wish me well at my appointment. *Seriously, what kind of busy professional cares that much to call the patient before they go in for a biopsy?* "Oh, while I have you on the phone," I said, "Could we get a referral for Darlene to see Dr. M?"

Of course, he agreed. **How lucky were we!**

We became quite famous from this incident. Every time we returned to the Calgary hospital, we were introduced to others; "You know those two ladies I told you about" and "Oh yeah I remember!"

While my biopsy was being done, Darlene was getting her x-ray and a cast on her fractured leg. She didn't end up needing surgery, just a cast – and we ended up being done at exactly the same time.

*You just can't make this sh#t up, can you?*

a thought

"Miracles
Do
happen!"

# 14 COGS AND SCREWS

A day or so after the biopsy in Calgary, I got the call saying that it was indeed a sarcoma in my leg, and thus began my journey as a "cog in the wheel" of the Cancer Machine.

Once we found out that I had cancer, I was required to do 72 hours of continuous chemo and then radiation, even though the success rate is about 0%. They don't know what else to do, because they have had such little success with sarcomas in the past.

I reached out to a naturopathic oncologist in Calgary named Dr. Matt Pyatt and he was able to give me some alternative treatments. These included Vitamin C therapies and hyperthermia, in conjunction with prayer, wheatgrass and essential oils. This actually ended up shrinking my tumor by 25% in the next six weeks (which is unheard of). In the report from the doctor, you could tell that even he was shocked that the tumour had actually shrunk.

When I had to go in for chemo, Darlene was still laid up and unable to come with me but our dear friend, Heather, was kind enough to spend some time with me in the hospital. She also happens to be a nurse, so that was very comforting to me.

My roommate at the hospital was named Zetta, my cancer twin. She and I were always having some kind of competition and talking about this lovely rosé wine (that's what I called the chemo medication because it was such a nice pink colour, like a rosé would be) that we were "drinking," and saying that's why we felt so crappy; we were just hung over 😃.

I had aromatherapy going in our room and nurses would come by and say "Oh man, it smells like a spa in here," and they would want to come in and stay. Kind of funny, seeing that all there was going on was 2 people getting chemo.

During the chemotherapy, I looked at the little dots that were going across the screen and noticed that if I sat up, they went faster. If I stood up, they went even faster. So I thought, maybe I should get some exercise while I'm here. I ended up doing a 5k around the unit in circles, round and round and round. This made the chemotherapy go faster. Often during this time, I would be on the phone with my son, Bryce, negotiating the sale of an acreage we had listed; we managed to sell it for just under a million dollars. This energizer bunny doesn't stop for anything.

After we were done with the chemo I had to have radiation every day for 10 days, excluding weekends, which I did in conjunction with the hyperthermia. The problem was that we had to stay in Calgary to do this.

Darlene had a friend drive her down to stay with me, but neither of us could really go out, so we just stayed in the hotel. We had friends bring us food, because I couldn't leave her by herself for long with a broken leg. Like I said, you can't make this sh#t up.

Later on, there was a small window of time between chemo, radiation and hyperthermia and the actual surgery. It was supposed to be 10 days, but we managed to push the appointments a little further apart and have the surgery a bit later so that we could go to Hawaii, where we had just purchased our dream place in Kauai. Our goal had been to go for an extended stay of three or four months, but that wasn't going to happen. We managed to get there for 17 days and it felt like bliss.

During this time I was hoping that I wasn't going to lose all my hair. There was only a small chance that I was going to get to keep my hair, and I didn't realize what a girly girl I was and how important my hair was to me until I lost it all.

Our friend, Dr. Dianna Martens, a chiropractor, came to our house to give us adjustments. As she was giving me the adjustment, she held my head and my hair was literally falling out in clumps. She was so great, she didn't say anything; just kept on with the treatment but after that, I drove to the hairdresser and said to shave it all off.

It was very uncomfortable, and not something that I would like to repeat. Also, it is very cold not to have hair – the slightest breeze, even in a warm place, is very cold. So I was wearing little hats all the time, even in Hawaii.

I did go and try on wigs, but all that did was make me laugh really, really hard because I have short spiky hair, and they just don't make wigs that are short and spiky. I tried on long wigs too, and we got a lot of entertainment out of that, but yep, that wasn't going to happen.

I just had to wait for my own hair to grow back, which actually took a really long time. And when it grew back, it came in curly and weird, so I just kept shaving it off because I didn't like it. Eventually, it grew back relatively straight but I keep it short because it tends to get really curly. When it came back it was like new, baby hair. I don't think I had one hair fall out of my head for an entire year after it grew back. Now, I don't even dye it anymore. I've gone grey, and I'm just living with what God has given me for a hairdo and enjoying it.

When we returned from Hawaii, I had surgery. My roommate Zetta from the "chemo games" and I had the surgery the same day. She was 70 years old and I was in my 50's, but she actually "walked" out of the hospital after two days on her own steam, whereas I was in there for three more days as my surgery was more intense than hers (or so I tell myself, so I don't feel bad about a 70 year old kicking my butt and getting out of the hospital before me). She is an amazing, resilient, woman and we are definitely bonded after this experience. We keep close tabs on each other and look forward to times when we get to connect at our appointments.

They had taken out a large amount of my quad muscle. They had to get a cadaver Achilles' tendon to replace my IT band because the tumor had been wrapped around it. I basically don't have much muscle on the outside of my leg by my knee and up the thigh. You can literally feel the bone in the side of my leg.

The rehab was quite intense and painful but I worked at it every day, because I thought, *I'm going to walk, and I'm going to be fine. This isn't going to slow me down.* It took a very long time, but I got to the point where I wasn't limping anymore.

I thought things were going pretty well, but on follow-up CT's and MRI's something kept 'lighting up' on the bone. This type of cancer could potentially go from being beside the bone to inside it or into your lungs. It kind of travels around wherever it wants.

Dr. Monument kept telling the team who reviewed my case that he thought the bone was just angry because he had cut really close to it, taking off the periosteum (the layer that covers the bone) to get the tumor away from where it sat on the outside of my leg. His colleagues felt that a bone biopsy should be done to make sure the cancer hadn't returned.

The fellow that performed the bone biopsy was new to the procedure; in fact, I think it was the first one that he'd ever done. It was extremely painful. I was in so much pain, I was coming off the table – and I have a high pain tolerance, *and* they were even giving me extra drugs.

Ten days later, we were out at our place at the lake. It was a very stressful time, as we were trying to get our cottage renovated and it wasn't going very well. We were in the middle of cleaning up and Darlene said, "You need to take this dog for a walk." We were babysitting our beloved grand-puppy, Butters. I grabbed Darlene's rubber shoes and headed out.

It was only September, but we already had snow, and it was slippery. I was walking down towards the lake, on quite a steep hill. About halfway down were these giant steps made out of railway ties. Butters was excited to be out for a walk and was pulling at his leash; I slipped on the snow at the top of the stairs.

I ended up seven stairs down – it's a wonder I didn't break my back or my arm or my head or whatever, but I did break my femur in half, and my leg was literally pointed in a different direction. It was behind me, pointing sideways. I sat there and tried to straighten it back into place before realizing that was not the best idea, trying to make my sideways leg straight again.

So I stopped and called Darlene. She was back up at the house. There isn't always reception there, but there was on that day, thank goodness. So I called her and said, "I think I broke my leg." She cried, "No, no, no!"

She came down and called 911. I sat there for 45 minutes in the cold, under a blanket, waiting for the ambulance. I was turning purple, I was so cold. The pain was unbelievable. I've never experienced anything like it. The sounds that I made were more a guttural sound than a cry. It was beyond tears. It was beyond crying… (thank goodness for morphine).

When George and Anthony, my paramedics, showed up, they had to park way down the road and bring their gurney and equipment along the lake before coming up to get me. They took me to Ponoka ER, where we were greeted by a fellow who looked like Doogie Howser. Great bedside manor, though. I had been hoping my leg was just dislocated. *Yeah, that's probably what it is. It's going to be fine. They will just pop it back into place and away we'll go.*

He took an X-ray of the leg and came back and said, "yeah, it's broken. Like, really broken. Do you want to see a picture?" My left femur (the largest bone in your body) was broken in half!

When I had initially fallen, I said to Darlene, "you need to phone Dr. Monument"; he was the doctor that had done my cancer surgery. He was in Calgary, and my same paramedics ended up taking me there the same day.

When I fell, Dr. Monument wasn't even in the country but he said when he landed, his phone 'blew up' with all the messages from his secretary. Everybody was trying to reach him on my behalf.

It "just so happened that he had OR time" – he was pinch hitting for a coworker and was able to do my surgery. ***Miracles do happen!***

It was a very good thing he was available because my leg is kind of a "Franken-leg", and no one else would have been able to figure out what to do with it. He was even able to go through the same scar. He put in a titanium plate with 10 screws, and told me to start the rehab all over again.

So, I had just finished recovering from the cancer surgery, and here I was buggered up again and having to do extensive rehabilitation. I managed to get it at the cancer center here in Red Deer for free. They had just started this new program, and provided excellent help. I went back to the gym and worked as hard as I could to rehabilitate. I still have more rehab to do. I have a feeling there will be a few years yet before I get to where I want to be. I have a bit of a limp, but at least I don't have to use a cane much anymore, except on long walks.

So, to recap: I break my ankle, get RSD and have to go through years of rehab before I can walk again.[6]

Then I get cancer. Chemo, radiation, rehabilitation again.

Then I break my femur, and I'm still recovering.

---

[6] Bonus info: In 2011 a guy runs me off the road as I turn to avoid t-boning him and I run right into a light post and total my son's car and screw up my neck and end up having to do more therapy for that, but getting a free European holiday out of it from the small amount of money that I received as compensation for being trashed.

# 15 REAL LIFE MONOPOLY
## AND THE BLOODY INTRUDER

I had broken my ankle and couldn't do stairs. The two-story acreage home we were currently living in just wasn't working.

So guess what I did the very first day I could? After 10 months of not being able to drive? Yes, you guessed it, I went out looking at houses!

I went to the city and was driving through a new subdivision and saw a beautiful one-story show home. Immediately, I had a really good feeling about this house.

It had one of the most beautiful kitchens I had ever seen. There were not one, but two $10,000 feature walls. Lots of built-ins. It had the quality of an arts and craftsman home from bygone days. It had five TVs – even one in the master bath. It was fully furnished right down to the tea towels and cutlery. I was in love!

However, I knew it was more home than we could afford. It was initially appraised at over $835,000. I asked the Realtor if the seller might consider a trade; he didn't say yes, but he also didn't say no.

I drove back home to talk with Darlene about my plan: to trade 4 of the houses we currently owned for this one big one. Yes, this was real live Monopoly in action. Four "little ones" for a "hotel".

Darlene agreed it was a good idea, and I started negotiating with the builder. The negotiations continued for a month or more.

Darlene was getting tired of the process. At one point, Bryce was horribly sick and puked all over his carpet. *How can one person have so much in his stomach? Is this a sign?* we thought. We cleaned the carpet and the negotiations continued.

One beautiful, sunny, September afternoon, Darlene had just finished prep on a wonderful supper and then started the process of working with a huge bucket of chokecherries to make jelly. Bryce was upstairs finishing his first day back to school, and I was in Red Deer working, and had stopped to visit a friend.

Suddenly, I got a text: *When you come home the police are here, but don't worry, everything's OK.* That's not exactly the kind of text that you want to get.

I'm thinking *oh my goodness, what's happening* – Bryce had a new hobby of climbing up various buildings in Red Deer and I thought he must have gotten caught. I had told him he had to stop a age 17 because if he got arrested he would have a record, and then he wouldn't be able to be a Realtor.

I couldn't have imagined the real story...

Darlene was working in the kitchen when she heard someone come in the back door. She heard a man's voice say, *"This is why you should lock your door."* She looked around the corner from the kitchen down the short hallway that led to the garage. There stood a naked, bleeding man with a broom held like a gun pointing at her. He was shaking it at her, saying again "This is why you should lock your door!"

Darlene yelled up to Bryce, "Don't come downstairs, but call the police." Of course, being young and curious, Bryce came running down the stairs to see what was happening. He saw the man and wheeled around back upstairs to call the police.

Darlene and Bryce managed to get out of the house, and **luckily** they had parked the car up by the shop. They weren't able to get the dog, though. They pulled out to the end of the driveway and within minutes the police cars came out of town, sirens blaring, through the ditch and into our acreage.

Turns out this man had a mental condition and hadn't been taking his meds. He had broken into our neighbour's house, used their broom that was sitting outside their door and rammed it through the screen and glass entry doors. I guess the glass had flown all the way across the house, that's how much force he had put into this effort.

Then he had proceeded to our home; broom in hand.

The police were leaving just as I drove up the road to the acreage. I could see a man in a straitjacket in the backseat. I was glad it wasn't Bryce being arrested after all, but not thrilled with this outcome, either.

The intruder had pawed through the chokecherries that were in the kitchen with his bloody hands, so we had to throw them out. There was blood on the door and walls where he had entered the house. He had ended up sitting in front of our very large TV with the Xbox controller.

(How do you calm a crazy man? Provide him with a nice comfortable couch, a big TV and an Xbox, apparently).

We had to clean up the blood that was all over the house. A friend painted our doors, we washed everything and tried to make the place feel better but it didn't work. This was the final straw – or should I say 'broom-straw?'

Darlene said, "no more negotiations; we need to make this move happen." Her feeling of security had been shattered. I agreed, and that day I closed the negotiations. We moved shortly after into the lovely show home, and rented out our acreage.

No more nudges needed; it was done. 4 small houses for 1 expensive one. Game over.

# 16 GIFTS OF K'ANDERS ON THE LAKE

Everywhere we live, we always say *"We get the best neighbours!"*

There is one common denominator. It's us. We are the reason we get great neighbours. I know people who are always getting bad neighbours...

Hmmm, wonder why?

When we moved to the "castle" in Anders on the Lake, it was a gift. I felt like I had been bestowed the honor of caring for this beautiful palace. I felt like I was the owner of Downton Abbey, or at least the caretaker of it.

We had so much fun at this house. It was basically like an open house all the time. We had kids and adults touring through, and kids moving in. We had a Christmas event that we called "K'Anders on the Lake". We decorated the house in royal festive fashion, and invited all the neighbours on the street for a party featuring coffee, fresh cinnamon buns and other baked goods. It was so much fun, and a way of  building community and making closer relationships with our wonderful neighbours. We are still friends with a lot of them today.

Darlene and I were also married in this home. It's a 7000 square-foot home, so it had lots of room to host this event. We set up chairs in our living room and dining room for the ceremony portion, we entered via the giant spiral staircase in flowing gowns – it was a spectacular day. We had two ladies serenade us with cello and violin to "Anna's Theme" specially arranged for us by Claude Lapalme, the conductor of the Red Deer Symphony Orchestra. Then we had an amazing meal fit for two Queens, and to crown the evening off, a dance. What a great blessing to have a home that would easily accommodate such an event.

In the winter, people would skate on the lake behind our house. The stereo system in this house was so good that the outdoor speakers could be heard all the way across the lake (or so I'm told 😊 ). People would be slowly skating with their families, but when I would turn on the Snoopy Christmas CD to *The Skating Song* you could see them smile and start twirling and speeding joyfully around the rink. They would look up to see where the music was coming from. They would wave and laugh and smile. It made their day, and mine.

One of my favourite crazy things the house allowed for was for Cole and Bryce to have epic Nerf gun wars with all their friends. This would involve turning off all the lights and running around the house out of the many interior and exterior doors, shooting each other with Nerf bullets from their giant arsenal of Nerf weapons. They ran throughout three levels of the house, shooting from the upper bridge, staircase, you name it. Nothing was off limits! The epic music would be playing full blast as they were having the time of their lives. There are still Nerf bullets stuck inside some of the massive drapery panels today!

The boys had LAN parties in the theater room and in the basement with their friends (everyone brings their TV's and you hook them up to Xboxes, and the party begins). We held free real estate education events in the giant living room. We had baby showers, birthday parties, musical events. Each year we hosted the Realty Executives office party, complete with a professional pianist and wait staff. You name it, we hosted it.

One day, Darlene invited in a group of people who were celebrating their daughter's quinceañeara. They were out in the park behind our house taking pictures, so she invited them in to have their picture taken on the bridge over the waterfall in our backyard, and in the living room by the grand piano and massive fireplace.

Everything was going great, until one of the family members accidentally hit the old-fashioned key that turned on the gas to the fireplace. When I came home from showing houses and smelled the gas, I went into panic mode and told everybody to get out of the house. We hadn't known the key had been turned on, so it took a while to find the leak; we finally did, and opened all the windows to air out the place. Danger averted!

My kids loved Halloween and with their ingenuity it took on a life of its own in the castle. Our annual Halloween extravaganza developed quite a following. We had many actors (our kids and their friends) in black morphsuits that would run around, jump out from bushes, sneak up behind people and even grab their legs from under the bridge that was part of our backyard haunted house tour. We had rats that jumped out as you walked by, fog machines, scary music, giant spiders, cobwebs… it was quite the production. Each year the number of kids exploded as our event's notoriety grew. We had maybe 200 kids the first year, and by the fourth, we had over 550 kids and adults that would attend. It was so much fun to put on such a memorable event.

We even had events out in the park behind us. Bryce had purchased one of those giant blowup waterballs that you can get inside and walk around on the water. He had it branded with our company logo, and he would set it up out on the lake and give free rides in the giant ball. Oh my – the laughter that ensued as young and old bounced, ran, fell and flipped around like hamsters inside the giant orb!

This house was meant to be enjoyed by everyone. The gift of including people was the biggest gift that the house gave us.

*Homes always come with gifts; special things that only they can give. Look for them, open the doors to neighbours, friends and strangers – the gift is for them and for you.*

My wedding to the lovely Darlene (left).

Our son, Bryce, havin' a ball!

I always say to her,

"If you ever leave me...

I'm coming with you."

# 17 I MARRIED MY NANNY

Ever since I was little — I'd say from about age five or six — I wanted to be Superman. I would carry the little girl from next door around like a superhero. I even tried to jump off the fence and fly but that didn't go so well. I can still feel the thud of the ground coming up to meet me.

I had crushes on other little girls during school, and a pretty serious crush when I was 18. But *that's just silly, girls can't marry girls* – and in my day and age that was correct. That was not a suitable option for redneck Alberta, or really anywhere else for that matter.

The girl I had a crush on got married. I got married too...

I had always dreamed that I would have a family and really wanted kids so that seemed like the next right thing to do.
It wasn't roses and peaches, and I wasn't sure that I should stay married. Finally, our first son was born. Oh how I loved him and my life as a mom.

I had to go back to work when my maternity leave was over. I have gone through a few different nannies. I was determined to find someone who was "as good as me or better" at looking after my son or I was just going to stay home! Some interesting girls worked for me for a while, but ultimately didn't work out.

Then, at church one day, (yes, I met my wife at church) I was introduced to two women who had come to Red Deer to help plant a new church.

Over time we became friends and, eventually, Darlene came to work for me as a nanny. She was awesome! She had tons of experience and was so similar to me in a lot of ways. She grew up on a farm like I did, we are close to the same age, (she read this and said, "we're not really" LOL) and our moms even have the same china pattern! She loved music, and God, but there was one obvious difference between us: she was much better at raising kids than I was. If I had raised them alone, they would have been so spoiled you would have been able to smell them!

After the heartache of losing a baby, we were extremely excited to finally have our second son. (Shortly after we married, Barry mentioned that he didn't really want kids because he was with kids all day as a teacher. Many years later, after he saw how amazing ours were, he said to me, "we should have had more kids." I said, "Now you tell me! Can I poke you in the eye with a fork?!") Anyone who knew him was very aware that, for him, the sun rose and set on his boys.

At this point my marriage had been in a tough spot for a while. We separated after the birth of our second son.

Darlene and I continued to grow closer together and our heart and soul connection became undeniable and unchangeable. We were meant to be together. We did not want to hide but believed society and our church and family and community was not prepared for us to be anything other than "Dar and Penny." Our top priority was our love for the kids, and desire to protect them from any hurt. It was many years of struggle and a lot of pain; running parallel to just living our lives and raising the kids, serving in our church, and building relationships with friends and neighbors, before we could finally find our way out and get married.

Sadly, in 2010, day after day we would hear in the news about young people who were jumping off bridges, killing themselves because they were gay and not accepted by friends, family, or their world in general. One day, Darlene just texted me out of the blue: "Today's the day – we need to tell the boys!" We decided we had to stand up and come out and say, "it's OK, you're OK, and you don't have to kill yourself just because you're gay."

We thought, *if we don't come out and live our life authentically; how can we ask others to.*

Our friend's little ones used to call us the "Tanders" – she couldn't say her "K's" – but to them the four of us were always just "the Kander's": two moms and two boys; just a family, living our life like everyone else and so that's who we continued to be.

We totally expected to have our lived turned upside down; garage door graffiti, egging of our car and house, etc., but we turned out to be pleasantly surprised. For the most part we were lovingly embraced by people from every part of our lives; a beautiful bubble of love. Before we could tell our truth, we had to be prepared for any eventual losses we may incur and be sure we could handle it. Some of those tough losses and harsh words came. The pain was horrific, but despite that, we have never regretted our decision to come out. Our only regret is that we couldn't have seen a path through to do it sooner.

We were married on July 14, 2011, in our beautiful castle on the lake with about 50 close friends and family in attendance. (Originally we thought it would be six of us but our "love bubble" kept growing so big that finally we had to cut it off at 50 as that's all we could accommodate.) It was one of the most beautiful, meaningful weddings that we and many of our friends said they had ever attended. It was the kind of day you want to relive over and over again. We were so *lucky*!

We had to fight to stay together; we had to overcome more adversity and challenge than most people ever have to go through in their lifetime, and for the most part we did it alone. No "back door;" no "others" to confide in. Just us and our unwavering belief that God made us and loved us and was going to see us through!

And you know what? It was all worth it!

*I always say to her, "If you ever leave me... I'm coming with you." I wouldn't want to do life without her. She's the "someone I can't live without!"*

# 18 THE RIGHT HOUSE AT THE RIGHT TIME

After 4 years of fun, we sold the castle in Anders in only 32 days, for full price; that was the highest amount that a house in Red Deer had ever sold for, and in a third of the typical 90 days on the market for an average home, to boot. It went for $1.89 million.

For us, this was an absolute miracle. Homes in this price range were typically taking 1 to 2 years to sell – and not selling at full asking price when they did.

We decided to move into a beautiful condo. The kids had moved out, and we liked the idea of the minimalist lifestyle that condo living provides.

The condo was situated at the top of Michener Hill overlooking the city skyline, with amazing sunset views to the west. The space was only 1327 ft². After the castle's 7,000 square feet, this was a considerable downsize.

I had always admired this building, as it was one-of-a-kind in construction and location. It was made out of concrete, which is way more expensive to build with than wood, but makes for a very quiet building. It was the first condo building in Red Deer built specifically to be a condo, and not just an apartment building that was converted later on. At the time I knew of a couple of people that already lived in the building, and I thought it might be nice to move into a place with a built-in community.

I couldn't have known how perfect this location and style of home was going to be for what was coming next in our lives.

It was just 4 months after we moved there that my cancer journey began and Darlene broke her leg, so both of us were laid up and not very mobile. This condo proved to be just what we needed – there was not one lip or stair from the heated underground parking to the elevator and up to our penthouse, so being in a wheelchair or using a walker or crutches wasn't a problem. There was only one step into my shower; otherwise, it was all flat to the ground.

Thank goodness this hadn't happened while we still lived in the massive house. Just to get to the closest washroom in the big house would've been more than either of us could have handled. How lucky to have downsized at the perfect time!

We were also able to pay cash for the condo, so our payments were very low. This was fortunate, because I wasn't able to work as much with my leg out of commission, and I certainly wasn't able to show houses!

We took the extra funds from the sale of the castle house and put them towards the purchase of our dream ocean-front condo in Kauai. Initially the price was $695,000, which was at the top of our budget, but we got it for $625,000. A great deal, considering that in 2007 it had sold for over $1,075,000.

The realtor that had listed the property was carrying a $200,000 mortgage on it, which virtually never happens. In Hawaii it is very difficult to get financing, but they basically played Banker for us, so we only had to come up with the difference. *How lucky, right?* It was not only the best condo that we had seen (still to this day) and it was really the only one that we could buy with our terms. It was meant to be ours.

We now live in a 1040 square-foot house, which is about 300 square-feet smaller than the condo. It only has a small single car garage and half a basement. It is located on one of the best and only historic streets in all of Red Deer.

We love living here – it's a wonderful community, with awesome events like a yearly golf tournament in which the holes are situated in five or six neighbours' yards, and my favorite: 'The 12 Drinks of Christmas.'

The event originally entailed going to 12 different homes, having a drink and a little bite to eat and then moving on to the next. It is now reduced to 5. We stay an hour and then they ring a bell, or like last year's event, the appointed guide starts singing to signify when it's time to move to the next home. (That was their 29th annual event; I've been trying to get on the street just to attend this for probably 20 years).

People go all out – one neighbour had a wide variety of alcohol including warm apple cider, and the best part was that they had made tiny shot glasses out of ice in which they served Troubled Monk Saskatoon Berry Liqueur as we exited to venture to our next house. Others put out charcuterie boards of amazing cheeses, towers of pickles, cheese and meat, poutine fries, Mexican fare, and last year...a 70's-themed home with perfect vintage cocktails like Snowballs and Pink Ladies with accompanying disco ball and a playlist to match.

Within weeks of moving into this house, I fell and broke my femur and was laid up again. One of the initial drawbacks of this house was that it only has one tiny bathroom upstairs, but for me this became a bonus. I could sit on the throne and wash my hands at the same time. It is also a smaller space so it makes it easy to get from one place to another. So again, it was the right house for us for this challenging time. [7]

*It seems that God always puts us in the right house at the right time. It's nice to know that someone else is in charge of your life – someone who can see the big picture, when we only see what is out our front window.*

Our beautiful "castle house" in Anders on the Lake.

---

[7] That first year, I went to The 12 Drinks of Christmas in a wheelchair; nothing was going to stop me from enjoying this great tradition.

# 19 NAN —10 MINUTES A DAY

I have a friend, Nan, who is sometimes brutally honest. I love her and envy her blatant lack of giving a crap. She is also a brave parent who tells her kids exactly how it is. I told her we could all use the option of being her for 10 minutes a day.

At times, we all wish that we could say whatever we want for just 10 minutes a day with NO REPERCUSSIONS. It would be as if it never happened, but things would change because of what we were able to say.

I've often felt better and discovered truths about myself and others after practicing 'Nan 10 minutes a day,' or the art of being brutally honest. This chapter is dedicated to her.

*Without further ado and without holding back; Here's my 10 Minutes...*

**(Remember the rule, after you read this and carefully consider each item, forget that I said it – it never happened; because that's a thing... right?).**

- Tenants – pay your rent on time! Don't lie to your landlords; step up and be a decent human being. Don't whine when you have to pay to clean the filth that you left and blame the big bad landlord. Seriously, people! Getting to live in someone else's house who has invested hundreds of thousands of dollars of their own resources into it is a gift. Don't cause your landlord sleepless nights worrying about how they will keep your place maintained and paid for when they were kind enough to choose you to be their tenant in the first place.

- Clients, don't choose a Realtor based on the lowest commission. That's like choosing a doctor based on the quickest availability for an appointment. Look at the whole picture, not just one spot on the wall; that small item is not the focus. There's so much more to consider. Do you care more about how much you'll pay, or how much you'll net? I care about how much you net, and statistically, people will net more if they pay a higher commission and get their home sold faster.

- Don't judge another person's pain and think you know better than they do whether they're in agony or not. Just because your friend broke their leg and their leg doesn't hurt anymore does not mean my leg doesn't hurt. Just because most people get MS at a younger age doesn't mean that my friend is lying about her diagnosis of MS. Seriously, people. Think before you speak!

- Don't tell me (or others) my parents must have died and left me a huge inheritance when you see that I'm your new neighbour and living in the biggest house in Red Deer, because you believe there's no way I could have made enough money to buy this house being a single, female Realtor... Wrong.

- Be Loyal. To your Realtor (and other self employed people). Don't usurp their knowledge and time and then take your business elsewhere. We only get paid if you actually buy or sell through us. If someone has worked hard for you, answered your many questions for free, or helped you out please don't give their paycheck to someone else! Period.

- Being a Realtor is not an "easy job" if you're passionate about it. If you are great at it you live, eat, breathe and dream it. (This is why I am up at 4 o'clock in the morning writing this because I'm worried about my listings, my clients and what I can do better to help them sell their homes). If you lived in my skin and walked my truth, you may, at times, feel crazy and wonder why anyone would want to do this job. We don't do it because we have to. We can't imagine doing anything else. It's an addiction, not a logical choice. We are in too deep, we will never recover; there is no *RA* or Real Estate Anonymous – we are in it for life. It's not a profession one chooses to make a quick buck.

- Being gay isn't a choice. If it was, then when did you choose to be straight?

- People, pull your head out of your arse and love your spouse. All in, all the time, with all you have. No exit plan; you have to be all in or be all out – you can't be "half-pregnant".

- Be kind to the homeless; remember, they are someone's son or daughter. How would you want your child to be treated if they were homeless?

- Take time for your children, buy a smaller or more affordable house if you need to. Don't work so much if you can manage. Kids would always rather have more mommy than more money.

- Don't comment negatively on people's hair or ask them if they are a boy or a girl. What difference does it make? Think inside your head – you don't need to say everything out loud. That's why God gave us thoughts. One big brain and one smaller mouth.

- Don't fight if you get divorced. Give the other person more than they are entitled to. Your children are watching! You aren't going to miss the money or regret being kind. It's already hard enough. You loved them once; remember that, and stop the madness.

- If you don't love your job, find one that you do love. Don't ruin somebody's day being grumpy because you don't like your job.

- If you believe there's only one way to load a dishwasher then you may have to be the only one to do it. Life might be easier for others.

- When there is a pandemic, you need to follow all the guidelines. Don't point fingers at everyone else. You need to self-quarantine if there is a minute chance that you have been exposed to the virus, or if you have been traveling abroad. Don't think that the people that are coming from a nice sunny place are somehow all sick. They are not; they are probably healthier than you. They want to stay away from you just as much as you want to stay away from them. The 6-foot rule applies to everyone. Not just those other guys. Don't get in someone's face or space when we're supposed to be social distancing. Come on people, let's all work together and get things under control. Be part of the solution, not the problem!

"Don't judge another person's pain
and think you know better than they do"

a 🪙 thought

"kids would rather have...

more mommy than more money."

"Be part of the solution,
not the problem"

a  thought

# 20 LISTEN FOR THE BELL: LESSONS IN LIVING

Bryce once met a young guy through his church, whose name was Matt Bell. He was a very clever and interesting character.

Matt knew a ton about marketing, videos and blogging. He also wanted to learn about real estate, and how to invest in it. He would spend days at our house talking with us, or even just listening to our daily conversations with clients. He had definite opinions, and was quick to tell me if there was something with which he didn't agree. Truthfully, this was a bit annoying at the time. He just didn't pull any punches and told it like it was.

Matt had given up a really good job in marketing, as he wanted to branch out and do more of what he wanted – life; without any strings to hold him back. He headed out on his own to explore his passions: video production and blogging. He sold almost all his worldly possessions and loaded up his car, rented out his house and hit the road.

He drove down to the States to hear Seth Godin, the author of *The Purple Cow*, speak at a conference. The book is about how you need to stand out and do things differently in business in order to be heard over the noise of constant advertising. Matt was kind enough to bring me back an autographed copy that said "Penny, listen to Matt!"[8]

He travelled the country, staying with people that he had met at conferences. They were like-minded individuals with whom he had connected, and were happy to open their homes to him. If he didn't have a place to stay, he would just sleep in his car.

I always thought what a great idea it was to just up and follow your dreams. If you know your dream, or have a place you want to be, don't let life hold you back.

A few months went by and I hadn't heard much from Matt. Then I saw on Facebook one day that he had passed away peacefully in his sleep.

What? This kid was only 35 years old...

I attended the funeral, where I found out that he had had a congenital heart problem and had received a heart transplant when he was young. He had known his time here might be short. He never mentioned any of this to us. He just wanted to be Matt... I guess he didn't want to be defined by his condition.

---

[8] We did listen to his advice. One of his tips was to create videos to reach our audience, which we continue to do today.

I began to understand why he was quick to agree or disagree with something. He didn't have time for filler. No time for bullsh#t – just the   honest  truth.

I learned from him to tell people if you don't   necessarily   agree with them. Enjoy every day! Live your dreams, do what you are passionate about.      Try  new things. Don't be afraid to fail. Just do it!

We could all stand to be more like him. So, next      time you hear a bell ring, think of Matt, and think *what am I doing with my life, and is it making me happy*? Because eventually the bell will toll for all of us.

**Enjoy the ride! Do what you have dreamed of!**

**Be like Matt. Don't leave this world with regrets!**

"Enjoy the ride!
Do what you
have dreamed of!
Don't leave this
world with regrets!"

a cent thought

# 21 GOD MAY ASK

*"God may ask you to adjust your standard of living to improve the quality of your life."*
*– Henry Schorr*

This is one of my favorite sayings. I was at family camp with our church one summer and the speaker quoted this. I wrote it down on a piece of paper, and I still have it today.

I have shared this thought with many of my clients. When people are hesitant about selling a big house to move into something more affordable – or as I call it, 'financially upgrading' – I share the benefits they will achieve, such as lower payments on their mortgage, taxes, insurance, and even utilities. But most of all I think that they should have less stress.

It can also mean the opposite. At one point, we chose to move into a larger home in order to accommodate our expanding life and the amount of people that were coming and going in our home. We had to adjust to a bigger payment, but the quality of life was better.

I always say, the older I get the more I am willing to pay to have less stress. If I have to accept a lower offer to get rid of a property that I no longer want, nine out of ten times I'll do it. I've learned that money isn't everything. Less stress and the flexibility to do what you want/need to do are more important to your life and to your health than you can imagine.

In life, if you have more financial and emotional margin, it makes it easier to handle things that come along – like broken legs or financial crises (or pandemics). We should always aim to live with more margin.[9] I'm sure you will live longer because you do have that margin. Just living paycheck to paycheck is much too stressful. Plan ahead to have some money in the bank and have some time affluence. Time to do what you want without the pressures of always having to work.

Plus, *the more flexibility you have in your life, the more availability you'll have to do what God may ask of you.*

---

[9] If you're interested in this idea, I recommend Richard Swenson's excellent book, *Margin: Restoring Emotional, Physical, Financial and Time Reserves to Overloaded Lives.* The idea of the margin refers to the white space around the letters that you're reading. If that wasn't there, it would just be wall-to-wall words and it wouldn't be very easy to read. You need the negative space (like less stuff or clearer priorities) to figure out what's going on.

"I choose to believe everything is a miracle!"

a 🪙 thought

# 22 GODINCIDENCES

Quote from Albert Einstein: *"There are only two ways to live your life. One is as though nothing is a miracle. The other is as though everything is a miracle."*

I choose to believe everything is a miracle!

Throughout my life, and on more occasions than I could fit into this book, I have experienced "Godincidences" as I call it, or coincidences, serendipity or whatever you choose to call it. Feels a bit like luck or fate, but it's often in response to prayer – it's the thing you didn't know you needed (but you knew you needed something).

For example, are you ever thinking about someone and then they phone? Back before caller ID, when the phone would ring, I would pick it up and say, "Hi, (person's name)," and it would be that person.

"How did you know it was me?"

"Oh, I recognized your ringtone...." Except, back then, there was only one ringtone!

Another example: when I needed to sell my truck because I had five tenants not pay their rent in the same month, and I just happened to run into a friend and client of mine who was in need of a vehicle. Out of nowhere, I had the money to pay my mortgage payments and maintain my excellent credit.

Or the time I was driven off the road by a lady whose car went out of control. My car had been driven off the road and onto the sidewalk, crunching into a pole. I went over to ask if the other driver was OK, and offered to buy her a coffee while we waited for the police. "Wow," she said, "I was just in an accident earlier this year and it was with a Realtor as well, but he certainly wasn't as nice as you."

Later on, I was looking at a friend's business and I had to go over to his client's house to talk to them about an offer. The husband opened the door, and the wife looked down from upstairs and yelled, "It's you! Honey, it's the lady I was telling you about, the one I was in the accident with!"

Needless to say, things went well and I was really glad that I had been kind. What could have been a crunched car *and* a lost sale turned into a new friend – that's "Godincidence" for you.

I have had times when I was so cash poor and real estate rich that I could hardly buy a cup of coffee. I needed to sell one of my houses, and fast, or the bank was going to be the owner of everything that I had. So what happened? I got, not one, but two offers on a for-sale property, and the second one was cash and closed in 2 1/2 weeks; just in time to save the day. As I always say, *"God is never late, but he's rarely early"*.

The same sort of thing happened a few years earlier, after I had broken my ankle and hadn't walked for 10 months. I was living off my line of credit on an acreage by the highway and they were wanting to expand the road by buying a small sliver of land off the front of my property. We had been negotiating back-and-forth for a very long time, but finally came to an agreement on price – and guess when it closed? The money *literally* came in the exact hour that I needed it. Everything was at stake! If I didn't get the money right then, all of my mortgages would start bouncing. I was in Hawaii on the phone asking the banker to walk the cheque for $259,000.00 across the room and deposit it in my bank account, fast.... Please and thank you! Talk about a close call. I was sure *lucky!*

I was living in a small house after Bryce was born. Again, a lean time; I was on maternity leave and a single mom. I would pray with my kids at meal time. I get really excited when things are at their bleakest because I know that God will come through soon, because the time is so close to when I need the money that it is going to have to be something miraculous. I prayed "Dear God, you know that we need the money in our bank account in two weeks and we have nothing in the works, so we are excited to see what you are going to pull off this time!"

The phone call came: a friend that lived in South Africa wanted to buy a house for investment. He gave me an idea of what he wanted and he said it would be cash and I could choose the house. This had never happened before or after this event. He trusted me implicitly. I went to work and found the perfect house and the transaction closed, yep you got it, in two weeks – just in the nick of time.

One of my favorite verses is *Psalm 5:3, "I wait in great anticipation for the morning."* I can hardly wait to get up in the morning because I know that something great is going to happen; it has to happen. It has happened before.

*Living life this way, anticipating God's provision, is the only way to go. I couldn't do this life without Him.*

Plus, it's more fun this way.

"Work as if prayer doesn't work, and pray as if work doesn't work". a thought

# 23 A WORD FROM GOD

"Life doesn't work that way for me," my friends sometimes say. But it can, if you are connected to God, and want it bad enough. As I say, **work as if prayer doesn't work, and pray as if work doesn't work.**

When I have had friends in the past ask me how I always seem to have work and money coming in when it needs to, I tell them the secret is my reliance on God and prayer. They seem to think that only I have this magical direct line to God, but I truly believe anyone can have the same connection. It can work just like that for you.

One year I decided that every day I would open my Bible to a random page, and I would look and see what word God had for me that day. Just a small morsel to chew on throughout the day.

I would open the Bible and the word or words had to be repeated three times on the page. Why three? I found that if God wants to tell me something, I often hear it three times. The first time is usually a whisper, the second is a tap on the shoulder, and the third is often a bash on the head. (I try not to ignore the first and second times anymore, as the third tends to hurt).

It was a very interesting experiment. Each day, I opened the Bible and, sure enough, every time – and I mean every time – there was a word that was repeated three times or more on those pages, and was exactly what I needed for the day.

Everything from "palm trees" when I was in Kauai, to one day it was "dead" – that happened to be the day that Reverend Billy Graham, a famous evangelist, had passed away. I didn't know that until later in the day, as I would do my word with God first thing in the morning.

Another time it was "40 years." I checked my calendar, and it was my 40th anniversary of being in real estate. God cares about every detail of your life, even your work anniversary.

Another was "father's house", and that very day we received an offer on the condo that belonged to my boys' dad. Freaky, right?

Check out the word picture of all the words I have received. **Trust me – God is real, and He would love to have a word with you.** ☺

# 24 THE POWER OF ONE CONNECTION

Back in the '80s, there was a publication called **The Shepherd's Guide**. A friend of mine was selling advertising space in it. I purchased a small ad about buying land and developing it, and included part of this verse:

*"They shall build houses and inhabit them; they shall plant vineyards and eat their fruit. They shall not build and another inhabit."*[10]

A short time later, I received a call from a fellow in Edmonton. Jim Dallin was his name, and he had a project he was working on in Red Deer. He connected me with an amazing guy, Charles R. Allard, and over the next 10 years I worked with them in selling an entire quarter section of vacant lots to builders.

Because of that ad, I was able to do something that no one else has ever been able to do in Red Deer, which was to persuade builders to pre-buy lots. Without these pre-sales, their project would never have gotten off the ground. The bank always needs to see sales before they will finance a project. That's the "cart before the horse" banker mentality.

How about "build it and they will come" *Field of Dreams* thinking…?. I wish banks thought more this way. But that's just the optimist in me, and that's why I'm in sales and not in banking.

This project gave me great insight into my talent for 'crystal ball' predictions. I could make these predictions because I discovered that the market always follows new construction. For example, if there is an excess of new homes for sale, the existing resale residential market will lag behind. On the other hand, if there is not a lot of supply or any new developments on the horizon, then the market is going to jump in the resale market.

I predicted just such a jump in 2006, and was aggressively pricing homes far above what other Realtors were asking. I ended up being in the top 7% of Realtors for Canada Trust, nationally and internationally. Canada Trust was one of the largest real estate companies at this time. I achieved this top 7% status for three years running, and continue to be a top producer to this day.

One year I came back from my annual winter holiday in Hawaii and popped in at a local builder's open house. He was selling new townhomes in Anders. I was shocked at how low his prices were and offered to buy 10 of the units at full price; but I wanted him to build my units last, and to build everyone else's houses first. I knew that by the time my units were built, they would have gone up at least $40,000 to $50,000 or more.

---

[10] (*ESV*, Isaiah 65:21-22).

He was puzzled at my offer and would have needed a large deposit to make it happen. I explained to him the state of the market and what I predicted was going to happen. He seemed to think I was onto something and took almost all of his units off the market in order to increase his prices.

Sure enough, real estate went up approximately one hundred thousand dollars per house that year. I should have bought them. Instead, I did what was in the builder's best interest and gave him the inside scoop. I can't help myself – I must educate!

Not all years were like these boom times. When interest rates were 17 ¾% to 22% we still had to sell houses, but we had to get creative. This was the early '80s, before anyone really did rent-to-owns, Owner Financing or even flips. I was doing all of the above back then. Now people take courses and join groups to do what I was doing 30 years ago. I giggle when invited to join certain groups, and think to myself that I could teach these courses. I've tried almost every one of these methods that they teach and have been doing them successfully for years.

I now educate my clients in creative financing for free. *Our goal at Team Kander is to make our clients wealthy. Not for the sake of being wealthy, but so that if they have more money than they need, then they can be generous and charitable and give away what they don't need.* This is our motto.

You never know in life what one ad might bring you, or that one person you might meet that will change everything. Keep your eyes and heart open to life's infinite possibilities. *One connection that could change your life could be right around the corner.*

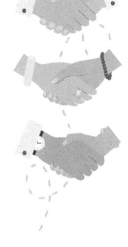

"One connection that could change your life could be right around the corner."

a 🪙 thought

# 25 ALIENS, HEALERS, AND TOUR GUIDES

Darlene and I have been incredibly **lucky** to become friends with many different and assorted people, but some of the most interesting ones come from our time in Kauai.

Our one friend, Kurtis, plays singing bowls, is an expert in oils, & does massage therapy. He has an amazing wealth of knowledge on many subjects. One night at dinner, when asked where he was originally from, he described his roots in detail which included the Lost City of Atlantis and a star near the Sirius constellation.
Well, that sure beats being from Innisfail, Alberta!

Another friend, Ricky, is a healer and an extraordinary human being. He has gifts and talents that are otherworldly. He performs healings as you sit in a pyramid-shaped structure that he constructs out of copper and is filled with Lemurian crystals. You sit and you heal while he plays his didgeridoo; the vibrations feel amazing. He sells crystals that have healing qualities as well as beautiful jewelry that is purported to do everything from helping you speak more clearly to lowering anxiety, or assisting with better sleep. When on Kauai, he often comes over to cook and eat with us. He is an amazing cook and an extraordinary musician.

Our friend, Set, was originally a tour guide for the company groups that traveled around various places, including Europe. We referred to her as "the Queen of 'The Cliffs'" – The Cliffs is the resort where we own our oceanfront condo. She was our downstairs neighbour for 4 years. Unfortunately, she passed away last year and she will be missed dearly.

Set spotted us one day as we walked past her unit with an armful of books. She was in her late 80's and loved to read. It was one of the things that she was still able to do in her advanced age. She had a knack for connecting people, and invited us to join in "Aloha Friday" held at her condo. She had a ground-floor unit so we could expand out onto the grassy area in front of the complex. The circle would expand to include all the people who would come and visit and connect – from doctors and lawyers, to nuclear physicists. We would all bring an appetizer and wine or whatever we were drinking and join in a time of conversation and laughter. She made "The Cliffs" a community, not just a complex.

Some of the best gifts from our time in Kauai; Bob and Sheila, both retired, renowned, Jewish New York doctors who have become some of our best friends. They are intelligent, down to earth, and a lot of fun! We adore them and they love us back! We have had the privilege of interacting with some of their family as well. The quality of conversation is like no other. When I asked their one son, who is a neurologist and researcher, "So, what's new with you?" He replied, "Well, did you know that there is a new scientific discovery called Yamanaka's factors? It is basically the "Fountain of Youth" and if you choose to participate in the trial, you may be required to sign a waiver that you would be willing to relocate to another planet because you could potentially live forever? If everyone participated, this could cause overpopulation on our planet". This was no joke. I Googled it later. This was infinitely more interesting than most people's response when I asked them "so what's new?"

As our one friend says, "in Kauai, you can throw a stick and you will hit a Realtor or healer". When I told my Kauai friends that we couldn't come because I had cancer, many of them responded with, "if you could just get here...."

Kauai really does have a powerful healing energy about it, and I would recommend visiting or living here to anyone. You never know who you might meet: a tour guide, a healer, or even an alien!

# 26 PANDEMICS, TSUNAMIS, AND MISSILE ATTACKS

It's never dull in my world.

I have been through two tsunamis in Hawaii. The first one was actually during the second last day of a trip I was on in Maui. I had thought about booking a fancy hotel down in Kihei the last two nights, so that we could be closer to the beach and closer to the airport. *Luckily*, I stayed put at my brother's place in Haiku, which is way up high on a 100-foot cliff overlooking the ocean, with no chance of being affected by a wave of any size.

Had we moved down to the oceanside, we would have been in the tsunami zone and would have been evacuated to the highest floor in the hotel and probably would have had to bunk in with the strangers on those floors like sardines. Instead, we sat quietly and calmly on the cliff, waiting for the wave to arrive. I was watching a whale give birth out in the bay in front of us. The wave did come, but did very little damage to the island.

On the second occasion, we were in Kauai, and another tsunami was headed our way after a 7.7 magnitude earthquake off the coast of B.C. We were evacuated to higher ground, as we were staying in a condo right off the harbour in a tsunami zone.

We ended up near the shopping center. It was quite humorous to see people camped out in Costco, sitting in the outdoor furniture section with their families, having a picnic with the food they had just purchased. We ate a lot of malasadas (Hawaiian donuts) and other snacks – you know, just in case it's the end of the world, we may as well chow down on the good stuff. But instead of a 7-foot wave, there were only 2.5 foot waves that hit the island – and again, did very little damage compared to the original forecasts.

Two years ago, when we were in Kauai again, we received a warning signal and text saying that there had been a missile launched at the island and that THIS IS NOT A TEST! My first thought was that I had just bought a new shirt yesterday, and I should probably put that on in case I don't ever get to wear it again. Darlene, of course, phoned the kids to tell them that we love them.

I also immediately thought about our downstairs neighbour, who was 85 years old and alone. So we went down and knocked on the door. I said, "Set, did you hear about the missile?" and she responded wistfully, "Did you see that sunrise this morning?" I repeated, "Set, did you hear me?There's a missile headed for us!" and her response was… "Well, what am I gonna do?"

I loved her attitude. I decided that if a missile was going to hit, I wanted to be the first one that the fallout landed on. We grabbed a coffee and sat out at the cliff so that we would be right in the middle of it.

It did end up being a false alarm, but it certainly shook up the island and made a lot of people think about things that were unsaid and undone. Crazy stuff!

Now, here we are in 2020, again in Kauai, and there's a pandemic of the COVID-19 virus. *OK, seriously!* First, they called for social distancing, then implemented a curfew, then they started to close the restaurants and businesses, and then our favourite supply of fresh food at the farmers market was also canceled. Within a few days they put the island on full lockdown!

We still had about a month left in our holiday, so we thought it would be safer just to stay in Kauai; except that our lovely government told us to come home. Not like we really had any choice – if we didn't come home soon then we wouldn't have any Covid 19 health insurance.

So we booked our flight home, and ended up with a sweet connection through Maui, then direct to Calgary on WestJet. With quickly unfolding events over the next 24 hours this turned out to be the very last WestJet flight off the island before they cancelled all other flights. *As luck would have it,* our lovely neighbour who lives across the street from us in Red Deer greeted us as we entered the luxurious 787 dreamliner airplane. She was the head flight attendant, so all the way home we were able to hear her soothing voice as we made our way back to Alberta. Plus, she brought us some lovely champagne from first class. Another sign that *I'm the luckiest person I know.*

Tsunamis, pandemics, missile attacks… What will be next?

"What are
YOU
Willing to Sacrifice

To have the life you want?"

# 27 PASSIONATE PRIORITIES

People ask me why I work so hard? I see it like this: **my job is to make enough people happy so that I can go to Hawaii.** That's my happy place!

In addition to working hard for my clients and constantly    sourcing new ones, I am also willing to sacrifice throughout the year to make sure that    I have enough funds to go on an extended holiday to Hawaii. I don't drink fancy coffees,    I rarely go to concerts, and I don't eat out as much as I'd like to. I don't buy a lot of clothes or shoes.    (Instead, I buy houses – ha!).

I am a bit single-minded, and I set my mind and heart    on going to Hawaii because I like to go someplace warm when it's winter here. When the kids    were little, I would literally sell one of the houses that I owned, if I needed to, so that I could    go to Hawaii with my children. Just the family, no work. I would leave my business with a coworker    I trusted and say "I'm going on holidays with my family. Don't call me, except if someone dies    – and only if it's someone I like." Because I worked so hard the rest of the time, I wanted to ensure    a fun and uninterrupted time with my children.

Now, with technology and with my son, Bryce, being    in business with me, he can be back home working, and I can actually work from Kauai. The office    is much nicer there! I can wear shorts and have a martini (when the work is done). I can    even work from the beach.

I love technology for the freedom it provides.    The better technology gets, the more time I can spend in Kauai; which would be the long term goal.    Quality service for our clients, and a sunny warm office with an ocean view for me.

**What are YOU willing to sacrifice to have the life you want?**

# 28 THINGS I KNOW FOR SURE

- Always marry up, and I don't mean financially. *"Don't marry somebody you can live with; marry somebody you can't live without."*
Just now, my wife woke up when she realized I wasn't in bed, and came to make sure I was OK. "My stomach hurts and I can't sleep, but my brain is bubbling over with ideas," I say, and she worries about me.
*How lucky am I* to have married someone like my wife: kind, smart, intuitive, loving, funny, beautiful... and she laughs at all my jokes and lets me interrupt her all day long and rarely complains. She would do anything for me, or for a friend.


- I have the best kids in the whole world. When asked about my children I usually reply, "Seriously, my kids are so great, if I could clone them and sell them on eBay I could retire tomorrow." They are smart, strong, brave, kind, generous and loving, and they are some of the finest human beings I've ever met. Yes, I'm tearing up right now writing this, feeling so thankful to be their mom.
Oh yeah, and my wife played a huge role in this. I have been known to say, "it's a good thing I had Darlene to help me, or they would have been so spoiled that you would be able to smell them from there."
People have asked, why are your kids so great? Well, it was kind of cheating; they had 2 moms and a hovercraft dad – they didn't have a chance but to turn out great. Hopefully, God will help them forget any mistakes I may have made; at least, that is my prayer. I love them to the moon and back, times a billion!


- God has never let me down and I believe He will always be there for me.
I have a childlike faith in God. Since the age of 25, I always have. He says he will take care of me and provide for my needs and I have seen Him do it over and over again. For the most part, I'm a *rose colored glasses kind of girl.* I just believe God sees the big picture and things will turn out ok; the way they are supposed to.

"Remember, money is not real...

Someone just invewnted it so they
didn't have to trade
a loaf of bread for a fish."

# 29 YOU'VE GOT THIS

Don't take life too seriously – look at it as a giant game, like Life, Monopoly, or Snakes and Ladders. A game of twists and turns where you have to find the solutions. Roll the dice, live it up!

Have fun; remember, **you are luckier than you think**. Think how **lucky** you are when you find friends and maybe a spouse who will hang out with you and laugh at your jokes? Appreciate them.

You are **lucky** enough just to be alive!
Seize the day. You were **lucky** enough to get to be on this earth for even one day; not everyone gets that opportunity.
Learn one magic trick, make goals, dream big, go for the gold ring – you can't win if you don't try.
Love your life. Remember, **you are the luckiest person you know!**

Move the game pieces around until you find where you fit. Find playmates who like the same games you do. Hang onto them; life is too short to do this alone.

Remember, money is not real... someone just invented it so they didn't have to trade a loaf of bread for a fish.

Share.
Help others win.
Find things that bring you joy, and do them!
Gamify everything, luck will follow you.
God's love will chase you down.

The cards are stacked in your favor. Don't cheat, play fair. You don't always need to win.
Play with kids who are younger and people that are older than you. You can learn something from everyone. Just listen and pay attention.

Remember, **you're luckier than you think.**
If, like in Snakes and Ladders you hit the slide, yell "Yahoo" on the way down! Find a ladder, climb back up; you aren't finished yet.

You can do this. **Life IS good. You ARE a winner!** You are loved. You are no accident. You are perfect. Yes, you!
God only made one of you, because when He created you, He was so overwhelmed with His love for you that He couldn't imagine making another

Life will throw you curveballs. Grab them and throw them right back!

Things will turn out the way they do.

Sometimes you can't do anything about it except believe that good will follow you. If you're tempted to doubt that, just look back at your life and remind yourself, as I often do... *I'm the luckiest person I know!*

## Say it a million times!

# I am
# the
# *luckiest*
# person
# I know

_____Is the luckiest person I know.
(your name here)

# AUTHORS NOTE

When I was little I loved flip books! Ever since I started writing this book I wanted to incorporate a flipbook into it. Now that you've read the book, you can take hold of the bottom left-hand corner and flip front to back to see my life summed up in a flipbook. If you are feeling down, just flip through as needed to remind yourself that it's not how many times you fall down in life; it's how many times you get back up that really matters.

Special thanks to Inga Gudziak & Oleh Kosynets for making the flipbook a reality. Thank you for creating the character, and for all your help with formatting, editing and getting the book to print. Finding you was another ..Godincedence..!

CPSIA information can be obtained
at www.ICGtesting.com
Printed in the USA
LVHW071946180721
693032LV00014B/338